Mary,
the Mother of Jesus

By the same author:

ALLAH OR THE GOD OF THE BIBLE –
WHAT IS THE TRUTH?

BEHOLD HIS LOVE

FATHER OF COMFORT (Daily Readings)

FOR JERUSALEM'S SAKE I WILL NOT REST

HIDDEN IN HIS HANDS

I FOUND THE KEY TO THE HEART OF GOD (Autobiography)

IF I ONLY LOVE JESUS

IN OUR MIDST – JESUS LOVES AND SUFFERS TODAY

IN WHOM THE FATHER DELIGHTS

ISRAEL, MY CHOSEN PEOPLE

MORE PRECIOUS THAN GOLD (Daily Readings)

MY ALL FOR HIM

PATMOS – WHEN THE HEAVENS OPENED

PRAYING OUR WAY THROUGH LIFE

REALITIES OF FAITH

REPENTANCE – THE JOY-FILLED LIFE

SETTING OUR HEARTS ON HEAVEN

THE BLESSINGS OF ILLNESS

THE EVE OF PERSECUTION

THE HIDDEN TREASURE IN SUFFERING

THE UNSEEN WORLD OF ANGELS AND DEMONS

YOU WILL NEVER BE THE SAME

Mary,
the Mother of Jesus

Basilea Schlink

Published by

chosen books

FLEMING H. REVELL COMPANY
OLD TAPPAN, NEW JERSEY

Copyright ©Evangelical Sisterhood of Mary, 1986

Original title: *Maria – der Weg der Mutter des Herrn*
First German edition – 1960

First British edition – 1986 published by Marshall Morgan and Scott
Publications Ltd, part of the Marshall Pickering Holdings Group, a subsidiary of
the Zondervan Corporation.

Unless otherwise stated, all Bible quotations are taken from the Revised Standard Version of the Bible, copyrighted 1946, 1952, 1971 and 1973, and used by permission.
Bible quotations identified NIV are taken from the Holy Bible: New International Version. Copyright ©1978 by the New York International Bible Society, and used by permission of Zondervan Bible Publishers.
Bible quotations identified RAV are taken from the Holy Bible: Revised Authorised Version, The New King James Version. Copyright ©1979, 1980, 1982, Thomas Nelson, Inc.,
Publishers, and used by permission.

Schlink, Basilea.
  Mary, the mother of Jesus.

  Translation of: Maria, der Weg der Mutter des Herrn
  Bibliography: p.
  1. Mary, Blessed Virgin, Saint. 2. Christian saints — Palestine —
Biography. I. Title.
BT605.2.S3513   1986   232.91   88-14952
ISBN 0-8007-9132-0

Chosen Books are Published by
Fleming H. Revell Company
Old Tappan, New Jersey
Printed in the United States of America

Contents

1 The Annunciation 11

2 The Visitation 27

3 The Nativity 39

4 The Presentation of Jesus in the
   Temple 53

5 The Visit of the Magi and the Flight
   to Egypt 63

6 Mary Accompanies Jesus Through
   Childhood and Youth 71

7 Mary During the First Stage of Jesus'
   Public Ministry 83

8 Mary Accompanies Her Son to the Cross 97

   Epilogue 113

   Notes 120

Mary,
the Mother of Jesus

1
The Annunciation

In the sixth month the angel Gabriel was sent from God to a city of Galilee named Nazareth, to a virgin betrothed to a man whose name was Joseph, of the house of David; and the virgin's name was Mary.

And he came to her and said, "Hail, O favoured one, the Lord is with you!" But she was greatly troubled at the saying, and considered in her mind what sort of greeting this might be.

And the angel said to her, "Do not be afraid, Mary, for you have found favour with God. And behold, you will conceive in your womb and bear a son, and you shall call his name Jesus. He will be great, and will be called the Son of the Most High; and the Lord God will give to him the throne of his father David, and he will reign over the house of Jacob for ever; and of his kingdom there will be no end."

And Mary said to the angel, "How shall this be, since I have no husband?"

And the angel said to her, "The Holy Spirit will come upon you, and the power of the Most High will overshadow you; therefore the child to be born will be called holy, the Son of God. And behold, your kinswoman Elizabeth in her old age has also conceived a son; and this is the sixth month with her who was called barren. For with God nothing will be impossible."

And Mary said, "Behold, I am the handmaid of the Lord; let it be to me according to your word." And the angel departed from her.

Luke 1:26-38

It may well have been in a quiet hour of prayer that

the incredible tidings reached Mary's ears. Never before had the earth heard anything like it: God wanted to descend upon this earth and visit the sons of men, but not as He used to visit Adam and Eve long ago in the Garden of Eden in the cool of the day. No, He wanted to become a human being on this earth. And from among millions of people He singled out one in whose womb He would place Him, who is of the same substance as the Father. There His Son was to develop as a human infant and come to us in this way — akin to us and of our flesh and blood. What graciousness of God! How close the eternal God wants to draw to us human beings, uniting Himself with us!

And who was the chosen one, she who was favoured of God before all other women? Mary. The tidings were delivered to her by God's messenger Gabriel, a radiant angelic chief prince, commonly thought to be one of the seven angels standing in attendance upon God before His holy throne. Drawing near to her, he greeted her with the words, "Rejoice, highly favoured one, the Lord is with you; blessed are you among women"(Luke 1:28 RAV). A human being favoured with divine grace, a chosen one of the Lord — this is how Holy Scripture depicts Mary for us.

The heavenly world would have taken great interest in this event. A dwelling was to be prepared for the only begotten Son of God, an abode for His divine Person. To whom would God entrust His Dearest, His only begotten Son, who was to be conceived in a virgin's womb? Beneath whose heart would His Son assume human flesh as a tiny infant, even bearing some resemblance to His mother? In great love the heavenly Father must have planned this calling long before the world began.

What awe and wonder must have swept through the ranks of angels and archangels the moment God made known His choice! The name of Mary would have been on the lips of all. Angels were not given the privilege of being a dwelling-place for God. A human being, Mary, the favoured one, had the privilege of receiving Him. What a high calling to bring to the world the very source of life — Jesus Christ, the Son of God!

"Blessed are you among women!" This is how God greeted her through the angel. After the curse came upon us through Eve, Mary was singled out to bear Christ the Saviour, through whom grace would come to us. Eve was destined to be the mother of all human beings, who were to dwell with God in His paradise and have dominion over the earth. By her disobedience she forfeited her vocation and became the mother of the lost, for with her No to God's command the gates of paradise were closed to us all. Would a No come for the second time from the lips of a woman, thus preventing the coming of Him who was to open the gates of paradise for us? Or would God be able to evoke in Mary a Yes and make her a favoured one, through whom He could give the world its Saviour, His Son, who as the second Adam would re-open paradise for us?

A message that involves a calling cannot come true unless it is received with faith; nor can a calling materialize without the assent of the one called. All of heaven would have waited in suspense for this response. Unlike Eve, Mary was not merely expected to obey a command of God. No, here God was requiring something exceptional of a person. A highly unusual leading, a special calling, was announced to Mary. A child, the Son of God, was to be born of her, and this was to happen not through the agency of a man but through the power of the Holy Spirit. One is almost tempted to think that it would have been more comprehensible had the answer been No. For do we not have greater freedom to accept or reject an offer than a command? When a special calling is announced to us, it is in a sense being offered to us. And was not the calling God had singled her out for an incomprehensible one — contrary to all His usual laws and leadings for us human beings here on earth?

More was expected of Mary than of Eve, who only had to believe that the commandments of God are good and right, inspired by love — and so too His prohibitions. Never before had a person been required to believe what Mary was supposed to believe: that God would overrule His laws of nature concerning conception and birth and, in the manner foretold by the angel, assume human flesh in her. What an impossibility!

Mary, more than anyone else, was required to believe in a promise of God in defiance of all human reason. What we are required to believe, others have believed before: that God can change people and circumstances, heal the sick, bring about a solution in seemingly hopeless situations. Such faith is exercised on a level within our reach. And every now and then God has been able to glorify Himself through someone's great faith, which extended beyond this level. The faith of a man like Abraham is a shining example. Taking his stand on God's promise, Abraham reckoned with the fact that God calls into existence that which does not exist and can cause a son to be conceived in a barren womb, just as Hannah and Elizabeth experienced later. But what Mary was required to believe had never occurred before. God

Himself, the holy, eternal God, was to come into the world through her, a human being. To believe this was diametrically opposed to human reason.

A unique faith was required of her. To believe in a doctrine would not have been so difficult, although nowadays many find it difficult enough to believe in the virgin birth, the event foretold at the annunciation and attested in the Gospels. They find it hard, although Holy Scripture, which teaches us to believe this, has been proven by God to be true: down through the ages so many other scriptural prophecies of grace and judgment have been fulfilled. But Mary had to believe for herself that this unique miracle would take place within her and through her. At the same time she had to commit herself to following this path and to bearing all the consequences involved — and that was the hardest part. No one else has had to take such a leap in the dark. Just how much this act of faith must have cost her we can only guess. Sarah laughed when God said that she would bear a child in her old age. But what God required Mary to believe was far more impossible.

This path of faith demanded exceptional courage and determination on Mary's part. And there was no one with whom she could talk, no one who could give her advice. She found herself far removed from every sphere of human experience. All she could do was cleave to God, to whom she was bound by the promise. Seeing that God was to be born of her as a human child, it was only natural that she should find satisfaction in Him alone and that she should turn to the Holy Spirit as her sole Refuge and Counsellor.

Indeed, an unprecedented faith was required of Mary in response to the angel's message. Now this faith had to prove itself in an unconditional surrender to God. It would not have cost Eve much to obey God's command. She merely had to resist the desire for the fruit of the tree that "was a delight to the eyes" and thus resist the desire to be like God. But how much it would cost Mary to comply with what God said! For her, obedience towards God would mean a life of suffering. Yet how could it be otherwise? Since the fall of Eve, God in His love is obliged to lead us through many trials and sorrows if He is to achieve His objective with us. But with Mary even more was involved. She was to give birth to the Man of Sorrows, who was destined to tread the path of sorrows for our sakes. As mother of our Lord would she not share His path? Thus she was called to a life of disgrace, scorn, loneliness, humiliation, poverty, and homelessness.

Would Mary give her consent? She knew that death by stoning was the punishment for women who were with child outside of marriage and thus guilty of adultery (Leviticus 20:10; John 8:5). She knew that Joseph would no longer be able to understand her, try though he might, and she would probably lose his affection. Indeed, he would have to part with her because of this law. She knew that this path would lead her along a precipice and that she would be entirely dependent upon God to bring her through with special divine help. Without His assistance she would be lost.

Would she have a Yes to such a path? "And Mary said, 'Behold, I am the handmaid of the Lord; let it be to me according to your word'" (Luke 1:38). Well might the heavens have resounded with that holy Yes of the mother Mary, a Yes of paramount importance for the whole world. With her Yes she gave herself unreservedly to God, expressing her readiness to be the handmaid and bondservant of the Lord for Him to do with as He pleased and as He had said. A Yes like this can be uttered only by a person whose desires and wishes are completely one with the will of God. This was the Yes of love. A soul that loves God cannot bear to refuse Him any wish or decline any proposal of His. It was the Yes expressive of a readiness to die. She did not flinch at burying her reputation, her hopes for the future, a happy marriage, or at the prospect of losing her home and all security. She committed herself to a way of life that would mean daily dying to self and to all personal happiness in this world. Mary gave her consent in such a perfect form of humility and utmost dedication that it cannot fail to move us deeply.

Her Yes included every area of her life: body, soul and spirit. We shall probably never be able to comprehend the magnitude of this Yes. There are heroic people who are prepared to make great sacrifices whether it be in the realm of the body, soul or spirit. But few are prepared to make an act of dedication covering all areas of life. Mary surrendered everything at once. God and His holy will were sufficient for her. There was no room in her for any hesitation or personal request.

"Let it be to me." This she uttered in the blind obedience of faith as she completely sacrificed her human wishes and desires, in contrast to Eve, who wanted to cling to her wishes and who, instead of surrendering her self-will, yielded to her desires. Mary committed herself unreservedly to this exceptional leading, whereas we usually try to save ourselves, not wanting to become involved with anything out of the ordinary. We are afraid of causing offence or incurring disgrace. The mother Mary, however, must have been free from all craven desire to please others and the fear of offending them to have chosen to tread this path, which for many would be an offence.

All she asked was, "How shall this be?" And after the angel's reply she requested no further explanation. Had we been in her position, we would have had a hundred and one questions as we sought pledges of divine help for all the trials looming ahead. Could she not have expected, for instance, that this little Child, the Son of God, would simply be presented to her one day? According to human reason that would have been the correct procedure and in keeping with the divine commission. Why did the Child have to be conceived in her womb? Why did it have to happen this way? From the very outset that meant a blemished reputation.

How utterly yielded she must have been to God to agree immediately to follow a path that could cost her a happy marriage, her reputation, yes, her very life! When we have to tread a difficult path for Jesus' sake, we know that Jesus will go with us and help us, just as He has promised. But Mary had no such experiences to go by. Only dimly could she sense that by surrendering her will and committing herself to this path she would receive divine favours and consolations, whereas the human distress that lay ahead would have been all too obvious to her. For the disciples it was a different matter. They were at least called by Jesus Himself to follow Him, and having Him right in their midst made their life of discipleship easier. Mary, however, received her calling only through the message of an angel. Apart from that, there was nothing for her to see. Her dedication was an act of sheer faith.

What was it that enabled Mary to give God her unhesitating Yes in that hour when His unique leading began for her life? Looking at Eve, we see that her mistrust of God made her succumb to the serpent's suggestion (Genesis 3:1-6). Not believing that God's command was inspired by love, she thought He was dealing unfairly with her. Mistrust towards God and His love is what makes us time and again rebel against God or argue with Him, and this mistrust evoked in Eve a No to God and His command. With her No, however, she incurred the loss of all the glory that God had prepared for her. From the very beginning of human history the love of God sought the response of love, which expresses itself in trust and obedience. This response He did not find in the first human beings.

Because Mary did not mistrust the love of God, she could reply in the affirmative. From the depths of her being she could sense who God is and what He is like, so well, in fact, that she had not the slightest doubt that what He said to her through the angel was good and right. As a humble handmaiden she followed this unique leading of His in obedience. A humble person can believe. Because he does not trust in himself or have a high opinion of himself, he has to look to God for everything. He who is conscious of his weakness will find that his eyes are opened to God in His omnipotence. Because of Mary's humility and dedication the great pleasure of God rested upon her. And this is why Jesus could be born of her. He would probably never have been able to assume human flesh in a person whose soul was not in tune with God but filled with rebellion and unbelief, as in the case of Eve.

Mary's Yes is all the greater when measured against Eve's No. We are indebted to Mary that God was able to use her Yes to cancel the disobedience of Eve, for through Mary the Saviour was born for us. This Yes expressive of utter abandonment and love paved the way for the coming of Him who would save mankind with His Yes-Father to a path of sorrows that would end at the cross. And so what rejoicing there must have been in heaven when Mary gave her Yes!

The annunciation also manifests something of the tender love of God the Father, for was not Mary's Yes ultimately in response to the love of God, whom she trusted? From the angel's salutation to Mary we see how lovingly God cares for a human soul, watching over it. True, God required something strange and unheard of, but at the same time He granted tokens of His grace. Mary, deeply troubled by the way the angel addressed her, by the great and yet incomprehensible grace these words signified, reflected what sort of greeting that might be. How immeasurably comforting the angel's reassurance must have been for her: "Do not be afraid, Mary!" Rich in mercy and compassion, God suffers with us when He gives us a calling that is linked with a cross and when He has to lead us along paths of self-renunciation and darkness. Along these paths we shall especially taste the Father's love. And it is this love of God that gives us the strength to say Yes to such leadings and afterwards to persevere.

If that which the angel first said to Mary seemed utterly incomprehensible, the promise that Jesus would be given the throne of David had a familiar ring to it. This was something she could understand, for the hope in the Messiah, who would ascend the throne of David, was alive in the heart of every Jew. Similarly, the reference to her kinswoman Elizabeth and the miracle that had happened to her was like a gentle helping hand of God. In His fatherly love He showed her the next step in this most unusual and incomprehensible leading, which had begun in that hour of divine intervention: she was to go to her cousin Elizabeth.

But before Mary went to Elizabeth she was granted the wonderful experience of divine grace when the Holy Spirit came upon her and the power of the Most High overshadowed her (Luke 1:35). The holy mystery of that moment is beyond the reach of human understanding, for no one has ever been granted such a mark of divine favour as Mary was when the Holy Spirit overshadowed her so that the Child Jesus would be formed within her as a human infant and she would give birth to the Holy One, the Son of God. A divine veil rests over this holy event. We can only sense that streams of divine blessing must have come flowing down upon Mary in that hour when the Holy Spirit Himself, the Third Person of the Godhead, overshadowed her, perhaps moving over her as He once moved over the face of the waters when the earth was without form and void. Who can tell what happened to Mary when she came into such close contact with the Holiest of all — yes, when the Holy One, the Son of God, assumed human flesh within her! When Moses was honoured with an encounter with God on Mount Sinai a radiance lay upon his features. What a divine radiance must have lain upon Mary, what a change must have come over her, when God Himself made His dwelling in her!

The tremendous effect this overshadowing must have had upon her entire being — body, soul and spirit — we can only guess. From Holy Scripture, however, we know that when the Holy Spirit descends upon a person, he undergoes a great transformation. The lives of those under the influence of the Spirit attest that the Spirit of God is a Spirit of great power, enabling them to do mighty deeds, as for instance Gideon experienced (Judges 6:34ff.). Moreover, He is a Spirit who creates good fruit in us, such as love, joy, peace, and patience. He brings with Him the divine nature, for is He not the Creator Spirit, who remoulds sinful human beings into the likeness of God? He imprints upon us the attributes of God again, in whose image we were originally created. But never before had a person been touched so closely and directly by the Third Person of the Godhead as Mary was. This must have truly made her one consecrated to God.

In the Old Testament we read of the priests and of those consecrated ones, who were set apart for sacred service. They had to keep themselves untainted by the world, because they were taken into the sphere of holiness. Time and again the Lord refers to them as being set apart unto Him. Those who had to do with sacred things were distinguished from the rest of the people. They were not permitted to defile themselves in any way; otherwise they would incur death (cf. Leviticus 21 and 22; Exodus 28). Their holy and exalted calling placed them under a special claim of God, as indicated by the words on the High Priest's turban, "Holy to the Lord".

Holiness was required in dealing with the holy things of God. But with the mother Mary far more was involved than rites and offerings prefiguring what was to come. She was privileged to bear Jesus Himself within her. After being touched by the Holiest of all, Mary would have kept herself pure in the spiritual sense, with her innermost self immersed in the stillness of God's holy presence. But even beforehand she must have lived in this state, for God usually prepares and trains His instruments long in advance, as He did with a man like Moses. How else could such chosen instruments of the Lord come into close contact with the divine and God Himself? He is a consuming fire and never draws near to us unless He has first cleansed us and purged us of our sins (Isaiah 6). He makes His dwelling only in humble hearts (Isaiah 57:15).

And so Mary must have been an especially prepared and humble soul for the Holy Spirit to come upon her and the power of the Most High to overshadow her. For does not the Spirit of God always withdraw when He is grieved? Great grace must have been at work in Mary's life for the Holy One, the Son of God, to be born of her.

23

O sacred hour and holy,
When Gabriel came down
And to the maiden lowly
His blessed news made known.

He came from highest heaven,
In glory bright arrayed,
Celestial splendour giving
The room of that poor maid.

His heav'nly salutation
To her whom God holds dear,
His holy, awesome tidings
First strike her heart with fear.

His gracious words amaze her.
"How can such things befall?"
The light and glory daze her,
She wonders at it all.

"O Mary, you are blessed,
For God has chosen you
To bear His Son, the Saviour."
How can this e'er come true?

And Mary bows so humbly,
Awed at such wondrous grace.
Giving her life completely,
God's will she does embrace.

The maid in simple reverence
Spoke those momentous words,
"So be it to me, Your handmaid,
As You have willed, my Lord."

The angel brought her answer
To God's most holy throne,
And through her willing "Yes, Lord"
The Son of God came down.

2
The Visitation

Now Mary arose in those days and went into the hill country with haste, to a city of Judah, and entered the house of
Zacharias and greeted Elizabeth.

And it happened, when Elizabeth heard the greeting of
Mary, that the babe leaped in her womb; and Elizabeth was
filled with the Holy Spirit. Then she spoke out with a loud
voice and said, "Blessed are you among women, and blessed
is the fruit of your womb! But why is this granted to me,
that the mother of my Lord should come to me? For indeed, as soon as the voice of your greeting sounded in my
ears, the babe leaped in my womb for joy. Blessed is she
who believed, for there will be a fulfilment of those things
which were told her from the Lord."

Luke 1:39-45 RAV

God's leading for Mary began with something joyful,
gentle, and supernatural when the heavenly world
drew near and the angel greeted her. But there is a
price to be paid for tokens of divine grace. The
genuineness of such experiences needs to be tested
during bitter times of inner conflict and distress — a
spiritual law for the chosen ones of the Lord, who
have been touched by the love of God. They are led
along paths where they experience unusual tokens of
His grace and favour but so too sufferings, trials and
temptations, which are just as great. This is necessary
for their spiritual refinement so that they will remain
humble and lowly.

No chosen one of the Lord has ever been spared

such inner conflict, not even the Son of God, who was tempted by the devil. The more unusual the calling, the greater the suffering involved. But never did a human being receive such an unusual calling as did Mary. Consequently, the suffering was very great. And by consenting to this calling, Mary committed herself to a path of suffering. To confirm one's election one must be prepared to accept God's leading, however unusual it may be, together with all its consequences.

But in His infinite mercy God takes care that His chosen instruments are not tempted beyond their power of endurance. He lovingly planned that Mary's visit to her kinswoman Elizabeth, whom the angel had referred to, would strengthen Mary's faith and confirm the angel's message. Mary, who was completely governed by the obedience born of love, immediately followed the angel's gentle hint. But even this initial step may have caused her sorrow. Perhaps Mary faced trouble in her family, who thought it strange that she should set out like that.

However it might have been, she was conscious only of a divine directive. Pleasing others with one's actions and leadings is of no concern, then. She was completely gripped by the holy obligation of her mission. And so Mary arose in those days and went with haste into the hill country of Judea to visit her kinswoman Elizabeth, who had also received a special calling from God and in whose life He had also done a great miracle, demonstrating that nothing is impossible with Him.

Mary was probably in need of a confirmation of her leading and mission. After the angel had left her, there may well have been moments when his message seemed like an illusion to her. What severe inner conflict must have assailed her as she considered more carefully the implications of the words, "you will conceive"! — "Conceive as other women do," she would have asked herself, "and yet remain a virgin? Who will believe my innocence? Who will take my side?" What disgrace, what anguish she would have to bear!

On her way to Elizabeth, Mary had to journey for many days across mountains, hills, and valleys, all alone with these questions. But in her heart she carried a blessed secret and hope: soon she would give birth to the Son of God; soon she would hold Him in her arms and gaze upon Him. What a privilege to bring Him to the world — the Hope of Israel, who would be king on David's throne!

Leaving Galilee behind her, she entered Judea, where the mountains are higher and the ways more arduous. As in a shrine she was privileged to carry across the earth the Lord and Maker, who would one day redeem not only mankind but all creation, making everything new. In anticipation of that day all nature may have shared in this secret joy, just as later it shared in the sorrow of its Maker at the crucifixion, whereas we human beings in our pride are usually blind to divine occurrences.

On the other hand the trepidation in Mary's heart would have grown the nearer she came to the house of her relatives. What would their reaction be when they learnt of Mary's great secret? What would Elizabeth and Zacharias say then? Would not Elizabeth misunderstand everything?

Then came the great moment when Mary, still a young girl, set foot in the house of Zacharias, no doubt feeling very shy of her aged cousin. And God caused a remarkable thing to happen. "When Elizabeth heard the greeting of Mary, the babe leaped in her womb" (Luke 1:41).

This God did to honour Jesus, the coming Saviour, through Elizabeth, who then said, "Blessed is the fruit of your womb!" But He also did so to comfort and strengthen Mary, who was called to follow such a hard path of faith and disgrace. Filled with the Holy Spirit, the aged Elizabeth pronounced with a loud voice words of welcome and blessing upon the humble maiden Mary, thereby lifting her out of her fears.

Here God confirmed Mary's calling through a person, who could not have known what God had said to her and what a wonderful secret she bore within her with fear and bliss. Only God could have revealed that to Elizabeth. Filled with the Holy Spirit, she said the same words as the angel, "Blessed are you among women!"

What loving-kindness of God! With this greeting He gave Mary the confirmation: the angelic salutation really was a message from Him. And so He strengthened Mary in all the fears and doubts that assailed her soul at the prospect of the shame and disgrace that awaited her. When Elizabeth said, "Blessed is the fruit of your womb!" a feeling of relief would have swept over Mary. This was no natural fruit that she bore but a blessed fruit — the very Son of God. For Mary it must have been like a new and gracious salutation from God Himself, confirming her calling and dispelling all her perplexity and inner conflict.

As Elizabeth continued speaking, Mary would have felt even more humbled by such a token of esteem. Scarcely had she entered the house when Elizabeth addressed her as the mother of her Lord, Elizabeth's Lord, saying, "Why is this granted me, that the mother of my Lord should come to me?"

30

How could Elizabeth show such honour to her kins-woman, so much younger than she? Elizabeth had become the mouthpiece of God, who in His infinite goodness inclined Himself to the one He had chosen to be mother of His Son and who strengthened her for the way ahead: "Blessed is she who believed, for there will be a fulfilment of those things which were told her from the Lord" (RAV).

Again, an answer to all the inner conflict Mary had to endure even at this early stage. Could it be that the thought had sometimes crossed her mind, "Had I not believed and given my Yes, I would not find myself now on this path which will end in ruin for me — re-jection, disgrace, and death by stoning! Could I have been mistaken? Was it just a figment of my imagina-tion? Did I have a false vision?" From Elizabeth's words, "Blessed is she who believed!" Mary could now derive strength and new courage to go on believ-ing for the dark pathways ahead when Joseph would learn of her secret and she would have to cause him immeasurable anguish. Again and again the words would later have rung in her ears, "Blessed is she who believed!"

And the words, "There will be a fulfilment of those things which were told her from the Lord" (RAV), gave her the assurance that this difficult pathway would not end in meaninglessness, stoning, the death of mother and child. Rather the Son of God would be born as a human being and later assume the throne of David.

Elizabeth was filled with the Holy Spirit and the flame of the Spirit also fell upon Mary, uniting with the faith that the Spirit had already placed in her, set-ting it ablaze. Indeed, on that occasion when two chosen ones of the Lord met, the Holy Spirit was

31

mightily at work. Both had experienced God's miracles and grace, and both were privileged to follow unique leadings for His sake. And so it was only natural that Mary should break out in a song of praise, the Magnificat: "My spirit rejoices in God my Saviour, for he has regarded the low estate of his handmaiden." We probably little realize how lowly Mary felt, how humiliated in the eyes of others, on this path of disgrace. This is why the honour shown by Elizabeth drove her all the more to her knees.

Unable to comprehend the favour bestowed upon her, she felt constrained to worship God. She could only rejoice at how gracious the Lord was and that He was mindful of her, freeing her from her doubts and confirming her calling. She could not but give praise that God had inclined Himself to her, who was not worthy of being so highly honoured by Elizabeth, much less of bringing the Son of God to the world. Sensing the glory that comes from pathways through the night of suffering, she was kindled by the Holy Spirit to acclaim the goodness of God in a loving song of praise, a mighty canticle, that we are privileged to join in to this day.

> My soul magnifies the Lord,
> and my spirit rejoices
> in God my Saviour,
> for he has regarded the low estate
> of his handmaiden.
> For behold, henceforth all generations
> will call me blessed;
> for he who is mighty
> has done great things for me,
> and holy is his name.
> And his mercy is on those who fear him

from generation to generation.
He has shown strength with his arm,
he has scattered the proud
in the imagination of their hearts,
he has put down the mighty
from their thrones,
and exalted those of low degree;
he has filled the hungry
with good things,
and the rich he has sent empty away.
He has helped his servant Israel,
in remembrance of his mercy,
as he spoke to our fathers,
to Abraham and to his posterity
for ever.

Luke 1:46-55

By His gracious election of Mary, God glorified Himself in this chosen instrument of His. He showed her favour and exalted her, and His name and actions were glorified through her life and canticle of praise. God is always glorified when people humbly consent to His call and follow Him in obedience, willingly taking upon themselves the trials and temptations that are bound to ensue. So why should we not say with Elizabeth, especially seeing that it pleased the Holy Spirit to speak thus through her: "Blessed are you among women, Mary, and blessed is the fruit of your womb!" As the Word of God shows us, to give honour in this way does not rob God of His glory, for with her canticle of praise, which sprung from humble submission, Mary actually magnified the glory of God. In humility and love she returned to God all the honour shown to her, keeping none of it for herself.

For Mary, who was carrying the divine Child beneath her heart, the three-month visitation was a quiet, holy time, rich in blessing. God had a purpose in bringing her together with Elizabeth and Zacharias. They too were visited by the Lord: Zacharias in judgment, for he had lost his speech because of his unbelief; and Elizabeth in grace, for God had taken away her reproach and given her a son who would prepare the way for Jesus. Together they would have searched the Scriptures for the prophecies about the coming of the Messiah and His forerunner.

Expectant mothers think much about their child: what it will be like in appearance and character, what its calling will be, and what path it will follow through life. But who can comprehend and imagine what divine thoughts must have filled Mary, the favoured one, during those months as she was privileged to bear the Son of God beneath her heart! The Spirit of God would have also spoken to her through everything else that the godly Elizabeth shared with her and He would have given her many a revelation about Jesus in the light of the Scriptures. Did she perhaps have an inkling even then that His life, and so too her own, would in every respect be one of suffering and under the shadow of the cross? However it might have been, she had given her assent, and this entailed an ever-new readiness to confirm her calling on an indescribably hard path where it would become evident what it really means to follow Jesus.

Heavenly Father,
We praise You for Mary, the lowly handmaiden, for her devotion to You, and for the way she promptly carried out Your will, setting out all alone on the long journey across the mountains.

We worship You, O Jesus, for allowing Yourself to be carried in a human body across mountains and hills that You created.

We worship You, O Holy Spirit, for so wonderfully seeing this chosen one of God through all her trials and temptations and for leading her to Elizabeth, another of His chosen ones, to be strengthened in her calling.

We worship You for the divine mystery surrounding the meeting between Your chosen ones when the Spirit's fire in their hearts merged and burned all the brighter, causing Elizabeth to break out in prophetic praise of Mary and evoking in Mary the jubilant Magnificat, in which all her inner conflict was silenced.

We worship You for choosing one of Your created beings, a member of frail, sinful humanity, for the great honour of being an abode for the Godhead — mother of the Son of God.

We worship You that Mary was privileged to be the empty, humbly yielded vessel into which you could pour Your grace.

Amen.

And so with Elizabeth, who was the first to honour Mary, let us say:

> Blessed are you among women,
> blessed is the fruit of your womb.
> Yes, blessed are you who believed,
>   mother Mary.
> Your example we would follow.

*

There hastens o'er the mountains
A maiden, noble, pure.
'Tis Mary, gentle virgin;
God's Spirit rests on her.

O wonderful election,
O holy mystery!
God chose this humble maiden;
Christ's mother she will be.

Beneath her heart she carries
O'er hill and vale below
The Son of God the Highest,
Who came from heaven's throne.

It seems as though creation
Rejoices with her now;
The mountains skip in gladness,
The trees in homage bow.

They all unite to praise her,
This pure and gentle maid,
Who carries their Creator,
In faith God's will obeyed.

She hastens to her cousin
In Zacharias' home.
She senses God awaits her;
What blessed hour will come!

Then floods of grace come flowing
And bring her joy and peace.
The Lord confirms her calling;
Her anxious fears all cease.

Her cousin by God's Spirit
Pronounces gracious words,
The babe within her leaping
To greet his King and Lord.

Such bliss this brings to Mary;
Dispelled are cares and fear.
She knows that God has showered
His highest grace on her.

Her spirit soars to praise Him,
Her God to magnify,
Who looked upon His handmaid,
Her sorrow turned to joy.

She's privileged to bear Jesus,
God's only Son, our Lord.
In joy she has a foretaste
Of suff'ring's great reward.

Anew her will she offers,
Not heeding pain or woe.
She knows how blest the calling
God has on her bestowed.

3
The Nativity

And Mary remained with her about three months, and returned to her home.

Luke 1:56

Now the birth of Jesus Christ took place in this way. When his mother Mary had been betrothed to Joseph, before they came together she was found to be with child of the Holy Spirit; and her husband Joseph, being a just man and unwilling to put her to shame, resolved to divorce her quietly.

But as he considered this, behold, an angel of the Lord appeared to him in a dream, saying, "Joseph, son of David, do not fear to take Mary your wife, for that which is conceived in her is of the Holy Spirit; she will bear a son, and you shall call his name Jesus, for he will save his people from their sins."...When Joseph woke from sleep, he did as the angel of the Lord commanded him; he took his wife.

Matthew 1:18-21,24

What may have lain in the months between the visitation and the birth of Jesus? Perhaps Mary's time with Elizabeth ended with the birth of John. When the angel announced to Mary that with God nothing is impossible, mentioning her cousin Elizabeth as a proof, he added that she was already in her sixth month. The Gospel of Luke also records that Mary stayed about three months with Elizabeth. But even if Mary did return to Nazareth before the birth of John, she was bound to have heard about what happened at his birth.

Once again God demonstrates for us in the life of the mother Mary the divine law that He never leads us on paths of suffering without first leading us to the heights of Tabor, revealing to us something of His thoughts and plans and equipping us with His grace and strength. This was Mary's experience. After hearing from Elizabeth's lips the Holy Spirit's confirmation of her calling and having been strengthened by the miracle God had wrought in Elizabeth's life, Mary received a similar confirmation through Zacharias. He uttered those words of prophecy that John was born to prepare the way for the Lord and Messiah, whose mother she was to be.

Now Mary had to leave the heights of her Mount Tabor and tread the downward path of suffering, trials and temptations. Though she had gone to Elizabeth and Zacharias with trepidation, she had still hoped for the understanding of Elizabeth. But on her way back to Nazareth her fear would have been all the greater: "How will my relatives and the neighbours receive me? What will Joseph's reaction be?" Indeed, the conviction would have grown in her: "Joseph will not be able to understand me. He will part with me. My relatives and the neighbours will point at me and not want to have anything more to do with me. Humanly speaking, I have nothing but rejection, perhaps even stoning, to expect."

It was a bitterly hard journey back to her home town, where she would have to endure the remaining months before the birth of her Child Jesus. Could she not have stayed with Elizabeth, hiding herself there till the Child was born, and then let Zacharias and Elizabeth testify in her behalf and declare who this Child was? But Mary went. She went in obedience to

40

God. Just as she had hurried to Elizabeth at the angel's word, now that the three months were over she hastened back to Nazareth in order to face all the ordeals that awaited her there.

Everything came to pass just as Mary had foreseen. Indeed, nothing save a miracle of the Lord could have altered that. She was found to be with child, and Joseph decided to break off the engagement quietly (Matthew 1:19). What agonizing thoughts and questions must have filled the heart of Joseph prior to this decision — what anguish till his fears were confirmed and he resolved to take this step! Perhaps talks had taken place with relatives or close friends after he received comments from all sides about the scandalous fact that his betrothed was with child.

Nazareth was a small place and did not have a good reputation. There were probably many malicious tongues in the town. How Mary must have suffered from them! What contemptuous looks and insults she would have borne when she but left her home to draw water or go about her daily chores! We have little idea how hard it must have been for Mary, because our laws do not impose the death penalty on a woman for having an illegitimate child. Appearances were against Mary, and since by law she would incur such severe punishment, Joseph wanted to dismiss her quietly, so that he would not have to report her. Nonetheless, this was no guarantee that her countrymen would not take her to court and punish her. What agonies Mary must have endured during those months!

God the Father did not spare His child Mary, the mother of our Lord, any trial and temptation. He did not reveal to Joseph immediately upon Mary's return that she was with child by the Holy Spirit. He did not prevent any misunderstanding on Joseph's part. No, first Mary had to endure the disgrace and reckon with Joseph forsaking her. She would have noticed what was going on in his mind, the way he averted his gaze and avoided her company. All her hopes of a happy marriage were dashed. She was forsaken, utterly alone, in her great plight. Not even the dearest person understood her in this situation. Almost everyone would have thought ill of her. Anguish of the soul and of the spirit, immeasurable inner conflict — this is what led up to the birth of Jesus. The cup of suffering had to be drained to the dregs. It had to be that way, because she was to be the mother of Him who was coming to suffer for us.

John the Baptist, who was sent to prepare the way of the Lord as His forerunner, also shared Jesus' path. He died a martyr's death; his message was unheeded and rejected, as were Jesus and His message. Likewise for the mother of the Lord there was only one path that she could follow, and that was the path that her Child, her Saviour, Redeemer and Lord, would tread and was treading with her even then, one could say, while still in the womb: the path of rejection, contempt, and disgrace. Moreover, if Jesus was subjected to trials and temptations, often being approached by the Tempter, then as a member of our sinful race Mary would not have been spared this suffering either.

Would not her soul have cried out at times, "Where is my God now? Why does He not make it known to Joseph that I have conceived by the Holy Spirit and have not sinned by deceiving him? Why does He not reveal this to all those who know me? Why does He not intervene from heaven and spread the word throughout Nazareth by means of an angelic message or dreams: 'Your Messiah will be born of Mary by the Holy Spirit'?" Yes, why not? — Because the path of those who belong to Jesus always has a special characteristic: it is a path of suffering, which leads to glory.

Yet in the midst of suffering God time and again comes to the aid of His chosen ones, seeing them through wonderfully. After those fearful weeks the turning-point came for Mary. An angel of God appeared to Joseph and disclosed to him that that which Mary had conceived was of the Holy Spirit and that she would give birth to a son, whom he should call Jesus because He would save His people from their sins (Matthew 1:20f.). Joseph believed the angel and did as he was directed, taking Mary home with him as his wife. What an act of obedience that was!

How relieved and deeply touched Mary must have been when Joseph told her what had happened! The fears and suspense in which she had been living would have been dispelled in that moment which marked the reversal of her great distress. After all the anguish of not being understood by Joseph, she saw him coming to her. He would not forsake her but take her to himself. Now she had a husband to protect her from reproaches and contempt. She had a home where she could feel secure. For Mary the greatest token of grace would have been that Joseph was not motivated by human reason or good-naturedness but that, once again, God Himself had striven for her by giving Joseph this command in a dream.

In those days a decree went out from Caesar Augustus that all the world should be enrolled. This was the first enrolment, when Quirinius was governor of Syria.

And all went to be enrolled, each to his own city. And Joseph also went up from Galilee, from the city of Nazareth, to Judea, to the city of David, which is called Bethlehem, because he was of the house and lineage of David, to be enrolled with Mary, his betrothed, who was with child.

And while they were there, the time came for her to be delivered. And she gave birth to her first-born son and wrapped him in swaddling cloths, and laid him in a manger, because there was no place for them in the inn.

Luke 2:1-7

As the hour of birth drew nearer and nearer, Mary may well have preferred not to leave the house at all so as to avoid the gaze of others. But God had ordained it otherwise. The Son of God was to be born in Bethlehem, the city of David, because He was to reign over the house of Jacob and to ascend the throne of David (Luke 1:32f.). For this reason God caused the census to take place. Arrangements had to be made for the journey, and then they set out.

Anxious thoughts may have arisen in Mary's heart as she wondered about how the birth would take place. Everything was so different from any other childbirth, for she was with child by the Holy Spirit. And yet it was just as if a human baby were being born. All this filled Mary with immeasurable distress and countless questions.

With this long and strenuous journey to Bethlehem, the Lord placed upon Mary and, no doubt, Joseph a new burden, for what a strain it must have been travelling for days across the mountains in that condition! Could not the Lord have made it easier for her, seeing that He was the Father of the Son that she would give birth to? Was He not the almighty God, Maker and Ruler of the whole world, with all things at His disposal? But it was God's plan for Mary that she should follow this path of poverty and physical strain, where her soul was afflicted with cares, fears, and many anxious questions: "What if the Child is born on the way?" and: "Where shall I take shelter? Where shall I find lodging?"

Elizabeth had said, "Blessed is she who believed!" But when God calls a person to follow paths of faith, he looks for something more than a one-time act of faith. He looks for a growing faith that continually advances into new territory; a faith that gives God the glory ever anew by trusting in His love in dark hours. Indeed, God wanted to make Mary rich in faith, rich in humility, rich in obedience. From that unique, all-decisive, initial Yes — "Let it be to me according to your word" — there came a whole series of Yes's, which were required of her in every new leading she had to follow as mother of the Lord.

When they arrived in Bethlehem, Mary's fears and premonitions were confirmed. Nowhere did they find a proper lodging for the birth of the Child, although they probably knocked at many doors and explained their plight. No one took them in. But it had to be this way, so that even before the birth of Jesus the words became a reality: "He came to his own, and his own did not receive him" (John 1:11 RAV) — nor did they receive His mother.

Could it be any darker? If it was dark in Mary's heart, it was also dark in the place that they finally found as a lodging: a cave. Perhaps it was one of those shelters for the poor, who would spend the night there together with the animals. Like an outcast, Mary was exposed, as it were, to the mercilessness of others. It was a foretaste of the pain and rejection Jesus would be made to suffer when He was cast

45

out by His fellow-countrymen in Nazareth and later by all His people. God did not spare Mary the anguish, for this is what Jesus would have to suffer in order to save mankind. The disciple is not above his master, as Jesus Himself later said. His pathway is our pathway. And His mother could be considered His first disciple, for from the very beginning she shared His pathway and tasted something of the sufferings He endured. All these hardships came her way only because she carried Him as a little Child beneath her heart. It was He who was refused admittance in Bethlehem. It was He who was exposed to the night and made to suffer homelessness.

Truly, it was night in every respect as they made their humble abode in that poor cave. It was in the middle of the night, not daytime, when Jesus was born. There in a dark cave rather than a brightly lit, cosy room He chose to enter the world. The night was not only dark but raw, for in the Holy Land at this time of year the temperatures often sink low and it is necessary to keep a fire burning. Yet even when dawn finally came — the days are shortest in this season — it was still night in the cave. Night seemed to prevail over everything.

In the soul of Mary it must have been night too, for where was God's help now when His only begotten Son was to be born? Was He really the Son of God seeing that God had withdrawn His help? Had she perhaps been mistaken after all about the promise of Him being "the Son of the Most High"? Had her experience of the annunciation been a figment of her imagination? The gaping expanse of the night seemed to engulf everything.

While it was night in Mary's soul and in Bethlehem, the eternal Light was to rise in that dark-

46

est and longest of all nights. Being the very Sun of heaven, It was to prove Its power to penetrate the darkness and illumine it like the brightest day. And so at the dead of night Jesus Christ was born — He who is the Light of the world.

Now there was light, for the Infant Jesus had come — not merely as a gift of heaven but as the One bringing heaven, for He is heaven's Centre, Maker, and Ruler, filling it with His radiance. It was Holy Night. That dark, sinister, gloomy, perilous night was consecrated, because He who is the Light of life, Jesus Christ, had chosen to come to us then. And Mary, His mother, who with her Yes had committed herself to following dark paths that were incomprehensible to her, partook of the miraculous transformation of that night.

Since that Holy Night every night in a person's life — every dark and distressing night for the body and soul — is ennobled and sanctified. To believing eyes it is wonderfully radiant with great glory and joy, for Jesus chose to come in the night and thus ennobled it. In so doing, He manifested that the night gives birth to the greatest things of all and that the light shines the brightest in the night.

And in that region there were shepherds out in the field, keeping watch over their flock by night. And an angel of the Lord appeared to them, and the glory of the Lord shone around them, and they were filled with fear.

And the angel said to them, "Be not afraid; for behold, I bring you good news of a great joy which will come to all the people; for to you is born this day in the city of David a Saviour, who is Christ the Lord. And this will be a sign for you: you will find a babe wrapped in swaddling cloths and lying in a manger."

And suddenly there was with the angel a multitude of

the heavenly host praising God and saying, "Glory to God in the highest, and on earth peace among men with whom he is pleased!"

When the angels went away from them into heaven, the shepherds said to one another, "Let us go over to Bethlehem and see this thing that has happened, which the Lord has made known to us." And they went with haste, and found Mary and Joseph, and the babe lying in a manger. And when they saw it they made known the saying which had been told them concerning this child; and all who heard it wondered at what the shepherds told them.

But Mary kept all these things, pondering them in her heart. And the shepherds returned, glorifying and praising God for all they had heard and seen, as it had been told them.

Luke 2:8-20

The shepherds were the first to learn of the wonder of that Holy Night, which saw the birth of the Light. They were living out in the fields, keeping watch over their flocks at night. In daylight they would never have been able to see the brilliance of the angel so clearly; nor would heaven's glory have drawn so close to them. It had to be night. Only against the backdrop of the night could the glory of the Lord shine forth so powerfully for them to see. In their hearts too it may well have been night, for nowhere are the wonderful tidings of the birth of the world's Saviour so joyfully received as in saddened hearts, darkened by sins and cares. When the shepherds then found the Babe, they could join in the angel's jubilation, for true praise arises most readily from the depths, from the night.

Indeed, it was as if this night and Mary's previous experiences of deep spiritual night had now brought with them the fullness of glory. The heavenly hosts came down, filling the air with their songs of praise to

God — music that probably no man had ever heard before.

Out of suffering broke forth gladness and rejoicing. After all the trials of the previous months, the joy in the soul of the mother Mary would have exceeded that of everyone else. Now the Promised One had come. There He lay as a tiny Infant. The shepherds came and worshipped Him, testifying to what they had seen and heard: the rejoicing and jubilation of the angels at His coming. And Mary, as Scripture says, "kept all these things, pondering them in her heart".

After the miracle of Holy Night, the way soon led back into the night of inner conflict. The shepherds' narrative had brought the heavenly world and its glory very near, but now this celestial radiance faded away to be replaced by the harsh reality of everyday life. It was dark again. In our personal lives we may have tasted something of this when after a special experience with the Lord we found ourselves faced with new troubles and cares. After childbirth Mary was required to stay at home for six weeks, as it is written in the Law. According to Leviticus 12:4, every woman giving birth to a boy was commanded to stay at home for a further thirty-three days after the child had been circumcised on the eighth day. This was the time of purification, which lasted till the fortieth day after the child's birth. And so we may assume that the mother Mary and the Babe had to spend all those weeks in the cave at Bethlehem.

Did Joseph have enough money to provide for the mother and Child during this period when he was not earning? This we do not know, but very likely poverty would have continued to accompany them. For instead of a lamb they brought only a pair of turtle-doves to the Temple when Mary offered her gifts of purification and presented her Child to the Lord. That was the offering of the poor. And what a poverty-stricken abode that was for Mary, who was confined for weeks to this dark cave! Yet what wisdom of God! Here she was completely cut off from other people and all alone so that she could devote herself exclusively to the Child Jesus and talk with the heavenly Father about His infant Son. The secluded cave was like a small sanctuary where she ministered to her Child, lovingly cared for Him, prayerfully and reverently tending to all her daily tasks there.

> In a garden there grows the world's
>   fairest Rose,
> So lovingly tended and cared for
> By Mary, His gentle mother.
>
> She cradles her Child, the Undefiled,
> A flawless Jewel so lovely,
> Endowed with God's pureness and beauty.
>
> With tender care she's always near,
> Whom God chose to be the mother
> Of Jesus, the whole world's Saviour!
>
> She kisses her Child; the wind whispers
>   mild,
> While softly the moon shines in wonder
> On its sinless Lord and Maker.
>
> The stars in their course all dance
>   and rejoice;
> The moon joins to honour and praise Him,
> While angels sing heavenly anthems.

Yes, angels are there; glad songs fill
    the air,
Unending Hosannas to Jesus,
Who comes now sin's power to vanquish.

What honour sublime to be the shrine
Of Jesus, as mother elected!
Oh, who would not call her now blessed!

So reverently on bended knee,
She worships in awe and wonder,
Yet holds Him and loves Him as mother.

O Child divine, Your coming's the sign
Of hope for man lost in perdition.
Your birth hails the dawn of redemption.

4
The Presentation of Jesus in the Temple

And when eight days were completed for the circumcision of the child, his name was called Jesus, the name given by the angel before he was conceived in the womb.

Now when the days of her purification according to the law of Moses were completed, they brought him to Jerusalem to present him to the Lord (as it is written in the law of the Lord, "Every male who opens the womb shall be called holy to the Lord"), and to offer a sacrifice according to what is said in the law of the Lord, "A pair of turtle-doves or two young pigeons."

And behold, there was a man in Jerusalem whose name was Simeon, and this man was just and devout, waiting for the consolation of Israel, and the Holy Spirit was upon him. And it had been revealed to him by the Holy Spirit that he would not see death before he had seen the Lord's Christ. So he came by the Spirit into the temple. And when the parents brought in the child Jesus, to do for him according to the custom of the law, he took him up in his arms and blessed God and said:

"Lord, now you are letting
your servant depart in peace,
according to your word;
for my eyes have seen your salvation
which you have prepared
before the face of all peoples,
a light to bring revelation
to the Gentiles,
and the glory of your people Israel."

And Joseph and his mother marvelled at those things

which were spoken of him. Then Simeon blessed them, and said to Mary his mother, "Behold, this child is destined for the fall and rising of many in Israel, and for a sign which will be spoken against (yes, a sword will pierce through your own soul also), that the thoughts of many hearts may be revealed."

Now there was one, Anna, a prophetess, the daughter of Phanuel, of the tribe of Asher. She was of a great age, and had lived with a husband seven years from her virginity: and this woman was a widow of about eighty-four years, who did not depart from the temple, but served God with fastings and prayers night and day. And coming in that instant she gave thanks to the Lord, and spoke of him to all those who looked for redemption in Jerusalem.

Luke 2:21-38 RAV

What a joy for the mother Mary when the time came for her to take her Infant to the Temple and present Him there! In her arms she carried a special Child, uniquely distinctive from any other, for this was the very Son of God. And now Mary was privileged to bring Him into the Temple, the house of God the Father. Would the priests, like the shepherds and later the Magi, see in Him their Lord, the future king on David's throne, the promised Messiah? Would the Lord reaffirm through them that her Child was the Son of God? From Holy Scripture it would not appear so. This lack of recognition from those who should have authenticated His divine Sonship must have caused new distress and trials for Mary.

For the first time the Babe Jesus, the Son of God, was taken to His Father's house, which should have been His real home. There in the Holy of Holies, where God the Father had made His dwelling, He could have stayed by rights. But not so. He was destined to be cast out of His Father's house. Here in the Temple precincts His people would even take up stones to stone Him to death in the very moment when He disclosed to them His identity: "I and the Father are one" (John 10:30).

When Mary took her Child to the Temple, she was probably not thinking that this was His home and where He belonged. She was merely complying with the Law. In memory of how in times past the Lord spared the first-born of the Israelites when the first-born of the Egyptians were slain, every first-born male was henceforth to be brought to the Temple, where he would be consecrated to God as a mark of thanksgiving. Because God in His great goodness did not accept this sacrifice, the child was returned to its parents each time, just as Abraham experienced long ago. Provision was made in the Law for the first-born of man to be redeemed. The mother was also to offer her thanksgiving, as well as her gifts of purification, and it is especially noted that Mary gave the offering of the poor, "a pair of turtle-doves".

Perhaps Mary and Joseph even found it hard to meet the expense of the two doves. Oh, little did Mary realize back then that her offering of two doves was too small. God required something far greater of her: her Son Himself was to be the offering. For the time being her Son was returned to her. Was she perhaps filled with joy that, unlike Hannah, she did not have to give Him to God and consecrate Him to service in the Temple? At that moment she did not know that three decades later she would be required to make a different but far greater sacrifice than Hannah, the greatest sacrifice of all. Hannah had to leave her son in the Temple, but at least she had him alive, whereas Mary had to sacrifice her Son to God when He died upon the cross.

Still unaware of this, Mary, radiant with happiness, presented her Son to the priests. Was He not the abundant reward of her paths of faith, a gift from heaven after her immeasurable suffering? But in that moment as Mary brought her offering to the altar, God the Father saw how thirty-three years later the true sacrificial Lamb would lie on the altar and suffer death. And He saw poised above the mother Mary the sword that would pierce through her soul when that happened.

On the Temple Mount one can see to this day the Rock of Moriah, where Abraham laid his son and stood, knife in hand, ready to sacrifice him. However, he was not required to deal the fatal thrust. His child was saved and Abraham was spared the sacrifice. Mary, however, would not be spared. One day she would have to look on while a spear would pierce the side of her Son. And a sword would pierce her own soul when she witnessed her Son, the only begotten Son of God, being slain by His creatures on the cross like an animal offering — He, the Lamb of God, the Guiltless One killed by the guilty.

In its deepest sense the presentation signified a sacrificial offering, and so it was befitting that at that very moment God should give the revelation about a sword piercing the soul of the mother Mary. He spoke through the aged Simeon, who made this prophetic utterance after praising God for the privilege of beholding the longed-for Saviour and after blessing the parents and the Child.

On the one hand, it was an act of grace that God gave Mary this revelation as she now began to accompany her Son along His pathways of suffering, for then she could continually prepare herself for the painful event yet to come. On the other hand, this grievous prophecy was like a Damocles' sword hanging over her, for she never knew when the sword would descend to pierce her heart. The words, "And a sword will pierce through your own soul" seem to indicate that she would not receive just one thrust of the sword, namely at the crucifixion, but that this sword would sink deeper and deeper into her soul.

This was to happen on the long paths of suffering that she would have to tread with her Son as she shared in His struggles and afflictions. If Simeon said that her Son would be a sign that is spoken against by many, this meant that He would be persecuted, despised, and rejected; and as His mother she would be affected every time. In the end the sword would pierce her right to the heart.

Since Mary's sufferings would culminate at Calvary, it was a mark of God's gracious leading for her that her trials began even before the birth of Jesus. Suffering continued to be the characteristic feature of her life, so that she became practised in suffering and would later be able to bear the greatest suffering of all, the crucifixion and death of her Son, in humble, loving trust towards God the Father.

Time and again in Mary's life, at holy, significant incidents, a message from heaven reached her to strengthen her on her path of discipleship and to kindle the light of a divine promise when it was night in her soul. So it was at the presentation of Jesus in the Temple. This time the words were spoken by the aged Simeon, who not only prophesied the sword for Mary but pronounced over her Son a promise almost too great and wonderful to grasp. Shortly afterwards the promise was confirmed by the visit of the Magi, which was a foreshadowing of the fulfilment of that promise: this little Child is appointed to be a light to lighten the Gentiles.

When Simeon broke out in praise, saying, "Mine eyes have seen thy salvation", Mary may well have rejoiced in her heart again, for her eyes could continually behold Him who was now being acclaimed as the salvation of the world, the Saviour. Indeed, her eyes were the first to see Him and now her gaze could always rest upon this Babe, who had been entrusted to her motherly care. The mother Mary would have been filled with new reverence for her Child at the message of the aged Simeon. The angel had announced that her Son would be given the throne of His father David, but Simeon now prophesied that He was "prepared before the face of all peoples, a light to bring revelation to the Gentiles" (RAV). Her Child's mission assumed ever increasing proportions, embracing the whole world.

From the way Mary and Joseph marvelled at these words (Luke 2:33) we can sense the necessity of God continually reaffirming the destiny of this Child. Whether He spoke through angels, shepherds, the Magi or Simeon and Anna, His message was each time a confirmation: "This is the Son of God and He has a mighty, universal mission, embracing Israel and the Gentiles."

The parents were in need of encouragement, because in real life everything was so different and most likely they were time and again filled with doubts. They saw that the Son of God was a human child like any other, born under the Law. He had to be circumcised and they had to bring an offering for Him. He had to share their poverty, their fears and hardships. His coming to earth did not bring them honour, wealth, and power. Of all the people they met day by day hardly anyone would have suspected or commented that this was a special Child, indeed, the very

58

Son of God. In their humility they would never have boasted to others, "Our Child is the Son of God!" Rather they kept this secret to themselves, hidden in their hearts. They might well have been filled with amazement, awe and wonder whenever God in His grace spoke to them through a person: "This truly is the Son of God that you are holding in your arms, Mary."

Thus the presentation of Jesus in the Temple brought the mother Mary both grace and suffering. God never gives the one without the other, for it is in suffering that the glory of God is revealed. So it was from the outset of God's dealings with Mary. The angel's annunciation heralded unsurpassed divine grace, which would also entail disgrace and scorn for Mary in the months leading up to the birth of the Child. Now once again God's message conveyed both supreme grace and profound suffering. Great and infinitely gracious statements were made about this Infant, causing Mary's heart to rejoice and exult. At the same time she would have been filled with fear and distress at the word about the rejection her Son would have to suffer and the sword piercing her own soul.

But as Mary envisioned this path of suffering, one thing must have helped her: the knowledge that she was privileged to tread this path with Jesus, the Son of God. She could leave the Temple with Him in her arms and always have Him with her in her everyday life as the source of all her joy and happiness.

Our beloved Father,

We thank You for showing us in Mary's life that when You lead Your chosen ones along extremely difficult paths, You strengthen them time and again by bringing them together with others, who filled by Your Spirit affirm Your leadings for them.

We thank You for leading the aged Simeon into the Temple when Mary brought the Child in. And we thank You for the comfort You gave him by showing him that the Consolation of Israel had come in the Person of the Child Jesus.

We praise You for Mary and Joseph, who obediently submitted to the Law and offered the required sacrifice although in her arms Mary carried Jesus, Your Son. We also thank You for deeming Mary worthy of being pierced in her heart by a sword, for by suffering with Jesus, she would also share in His glory.

We humbly confess that although we belong to Jesus we share so little in His sufferings, whereas Mary, as His mother, always shared in His sufferings.

Give us, like her, an obedient heart, a heart that endures in faith amid all trials and temptations and is loyal to You to the very end, so that our path of faith and suffering can be crowned as hers.

Amen.

See Mary and Joseph come bringing
The Child to the Temple today.
They bring the two turtle-doves gladly,
With thanks God their off'ring to pay.

In bliss, Mary, tenderly bearing
The precious small Babe on her breast,
Comes into the Temple for blessing
And holds out her Child to the priest.

Not yet does she need to surrender
For ever her dear little One;
The doves to the Lord she will offer
And take back with joy her dear Son.

O Mary, whom God blessed so highly,
Man's wickedness threatens your joy.
As hatred and jealousy gather,
Your Son they will seek to destroy.

Your heart will feel gladness and
      rapture,
But also deep grief you will know.
You'll share your Son's joys and His
      sorrows
And travel the way He must go.

The news with which Simeon greets you
Means both joy and sorrow outpoured.
Your Son will bring light to the nations,
But you will be pierced by a sword.

God's message you take to heart,
      trembling,
Though you cannot quite understand.
Your Son you will steadfastly follow
Till under His cross you will stand.

5
The Visit of the Magi and the Flight to Egypt

After Jesus was born in Bethlehem in Judea, during the time of King Herod, Magi from the east came to Jerusalem and asked, "Where is the one who has been born king of the Jews? We saw his star in the east and have come to worship him." When King Herod heard this he was disturbed, and all Jerusalem with him. When he had called together all the people's chief priests and teachers of the law, he asked them where the Christ was to be born.

"In Bethlehem in Judea," they replied, "for this is what the prophet has written: 'But you, Bethlehem, in the land of Judah, are by no means least among the rulers of Judah; for out of you will come a ruler who will be the shepherd of my people Israel.'"

Then Herod called the Magi secretly and found out from them the exact time the star had appeared. He sent them to Bethlehem and said, "Go and make a careful search for the child. As soon as you find him, report to me, so that I too may go and worship him."

After they had heard the king, they went on their way, and the star they had seen in the east went ahead of them until it stopped over the place where the child was.

When they saw the star, they were overjoyed. On coming to the house, they saw the child with his mother Mary, and they bowed down and worshipped him. Then they opened their treasures and presented him with gifts of gold and of incense and of myrrh.

And having been warned in a dream not to go back to Herod, they returned to their country by another route.

When they had gone, an angel of the Lord appeared to

Joseph in a dream, "Get up," he said, "take the child and his mother and escape to Egypt. Stay there until I tell you, for Herod is going to search for the child to kill him." So he got up, took the child and his mother during the night and left for Egypt, where he stayed until the death of Herod. And so was fulfilled what the Lord had said through the prophet: "Out of Egypt I called my son."

Matthew 2:1-15 NIV

Up till then God in His goodness had repeatedly sent Mary a heavenly greeting amid all her trials in order to strengthen her for further hardships. Earthly gifts now reached her at a moment when she urgently needed them for an especially difficult stretch of the way that lay ahead of her. These gifts were presented by the Magi, whose arrival had been planned by the Father as a token of His love. Their visit must have overwhelmed Mary, coming as it did, so unexpectedly and well-timed, and showering riches upon her.

But the gifts of the Magi would have been of least importance as far as Mary was concerned. For her, the leading of God behind this visit would have been of much greater significance. It was not that the Magi happened to be passing by their dwelling and, hearing of the birth of the little Child, looked in. No, God Himself had called them through the star. Far away in the East they had been given a sign that the king of the Jews was born, and the star had led them all the way to the cave in Bethlehem.

What a joyful atmosphere must have filled the cave on that occasion as the Magi from the East knelt before the little Child, presented to Him their gifts, and related to the parents how God had led them by the star! Mary and Joseph would have joined in the adoration of the Magi, and there would have been no end to the praises offered to God for causing the heavens to open and for sending down His only be-gotten Son. In Mary's heart the Magnificat would have rung anew: "My spirit rejoices in God my Saviour, for He has regarded the low estate of His handmaiden. He has abased Himself, and from my womb He has caused Him to be born who is destined to be the Saviour of the world!"

In spirit Mary would have seen her Son as the future king on David's throne, visited by the Gentiles, worshipped and honoured by kings and sages. Did not even Solomon receive such esteem? The queen of Sheba journeyed to Jerusalem to visit him, and all the kings of the earth held him in high regard. Mary did not yet realize that the angel's promise about her Child ascending the throne of David would not come true in her lifetime but many hundreds of years later and that her Son's life would turn out so differently. Nor did she suspect how much inner conflict she would suffer as a result — greater than anything previously experienced. All this was still hid from her eyes.

No doubt, at the coming of the Magi from the East her spirits were raised, and she was filled with hope as she envisioned the future of her Child. But soon the course of events would develop very differently than she had imagined. The Magi brought gold with them. For what purpose? Oh, she little suspected that in the coming days she would be in desperate need of the gold, because they would have to flee. They would spend many long weeks travelling to a foreign coun-try, where once again they would probably be with-out a lodging and have no means of earning a liveli-hood. Money was essential if they and their little One were to survive.

After the visit of the Magi, which was another

Mount Tabor experience for Mary, the way led once again down into the vale of tears. A new stretch of the way began for Mary: the flight, with death in swift pursuit of her infant Son. The Magi returned to their far-away country while Mary and Joseph upon God's command departed with their little Child into the wilderness in order to escape Herod's wicked schemes.

Refugees! In our times who has not heard of the misery of being a refugee or even experienced it for himself? If one has to flee with a new-born babe, the plight is especially acute. Countless numbers of these tiny infants have been known to perish on the way. But what flight is so gruelling as that through the desert? It is difficult to imagine a greater danger for a new-born infant than a trek across desert terrain under the merciless glare of the sun, and a greater miracle than when a tiny child comes through the ordeal safe and sound.

Yet this was the path that God the Father had chosen for His Son, who had now entered the world as a new-born Babe. It was to mark the beginning of His life on earth. A path fraught with hardships, grief, peril, and fear of death — this is what God had ordained for Mary, the mother of His Child, and for Joseph. Again the cross entered the life of Mary with great force. It was as if the Lord wished to show the mother Mary anew: "The life of My Son is characterized by the cross, and so your life too must bear the imprint of the cross, for it is inseparable from Him."

With this flight, God now led Mary through the desert in the truest sense of the word. Mary found herself, both literally and figuratively, on a desert road. For why had she set out with Joseph and the Babe? — Because Herod sought the life of her little One. And so in the desert too she could never be sure whether a group of soldiers and persecutors would suddenly swoop down on them and slay the Child. She could not know whether Herod had discovered which route they had taken and whether he would pursue them all the way to Egypt, for he was a king; he had great power and an army at his disposal. Undoubtedly, he would have succeeded in finding the Child had God permitted.

How often Mary and Joseph would have been startled by the pounding of hooves or the sound of human voices in the desert! They would have been filled with dread that their persecutors had caught up with them. The diversity of hardships facing them was great. First, they lived in constant fear of wild beasts, which are a particular danger in the desert. When crossing the desert, travellers normally banded together, for without the protection of such a caravan there was little hope of survival. Then there was the threat of marauding tribes, who roamed about the desert. Their anxiety would have been deepened by the sight of the little Child exposed to the burning heat and to the other rigours of the climate. And all the time they were haunted by the thought of starving or thirsting to death in the waterless desert.

Every time Mary was in distress, she had experienced that the Father drew near, giving visible proofs of His love. In the Holy Night the angelic hosts came down and the shepherds brought the tidings that this Child was the Saviour, the Son of God; then the Magi came bringing gifts. Thus we may assume that in the desert too miracles of God happened and that from time to time the heavens opened when the plight was most severe. Wild beasts may have lain down at the feet of the Infant without harming Him. Trees may have bent down and given Him their fruit. Indeed, God must have helped Mary and her infant Son, bringing them through in miraculous ways, for otherwise they would never have reached Egypt.

Such an experience would have greatly strengthened Joseph's faith too, for well might he have asked, "What Child is this that you have given birth to, Mary? Is He really the Son of God? Instead of in a palace or at least in the normal surroundings of a house, where He would be well cared for, God allows Him to be born in a cave. What manner of Child is this? Hardly born, He has to flee for His life with death on His heels. He is exiled from His homeland, which has been given to Him as King and Lord, and is forced to submit to the rule and power of another ruler, Herod, who is bent on killing Him. What manner of Child is this? Ever since He has come to dwell with us, we have had to suffer misery. Fears, poverty, distress, manifold anxieties and sufferings are now our lot."

And what inner conflict Mary must have endured at the mere thought that all those infants in Bethlehem would be slaughtered by Herod's soldiers for the sake of her Child! Oh, what anguish that must have caused her! How could she still understand God? But she went on following His leadings in obedience and, though not being able to understand Him, kept on trusting Him in the assurance that the ways of the Lord are good. All she could do was endure the pain and anguish of soul, but in so doing embrace and kiss the Babe ever anew, as we sing in a German Christmas carol:

Whoever yearns to hold this Child
And kiss Him joyfully
Has first to suffer with Him
Much pain and agony.

The flight through the desert was followed by the sojourn in Egypt. Did they find a dwelling-place in that foreign country? Or was it a repetition of their experience in Bethlehem, where they sought in vain for a lodging? We know how hard it is for foreigners to find accommodation and work. And so we may assume it was a hard and bitter time that they spent abroad. All His life the Son of God would tread the path of poverty, since this was how the Father willed it. As Holy Scripture says, He became poor. Being of low social standing, He enjoyed no special rights or privileges; nor did He have a fixed income later in life. During His long and exhausting itinerant journeys the Son of Man had nowhere to lay His head. All these hardships He endured even as a Babe, and His mother with Him, when they were forced to go into exile.

6
Mary Accompanies Jesus
Through Childhood and Youth

But when Herod was dead, behold, an angel of the Lord appeared in a dream to Joseph in Egypt, saying, "Arise, take the young child and his mother, and go to the land of Israel, for those who sought the young child's life are dead." Then he arose, took the young child and his mother, and came into the land of Israel.

But when he heard that Archelaus was reigning over Judea instead of his father Herod, he was afraid to go there. And being warned by God in a dream, he turned aside into the region of Galilee. And he came and dwelt in a city called Nazareth, that it might be fulfilled which was spoken by the prophets, "He shall be called a Nazarene."

Matthew 2:19-23 RAV

And the child grew and became strong in spirit, filled with wisdom: and the grace of God was upon him.

Luke 2:40 RAV

Instead of returning to Bethlehem after their sojourn in Egypt, as Joseph seemed to have planned, he went with Mary and the Child to Nazareth, having been so warned by God in a dream. Isaiah's prophecy was to be fulfilled in Jesus becoming a "Nazarene", an inhabitant of despised Nazareth.

And so the Child Jesus grew up in Nazareth under the care of His mother and father. In Jesus' day Nazareth was apparently a small place with few inhabitants and known for its poverty, its soil not being so fertile as in neighbouring Cana, for instance. But above all Nazareth must have been a disreputable place, just as certain localities are nowadays. We recall the words of Nathanael, "Can anything good come out of Nazareth?" (John 1:46). Not only did Nazareth have a reputation as a poor, small town, but few good and noble-minded people seem to have lived there, and accordingly it was despised. Perhaps an atmosphere of discord, strife, and malice prevailed. Today when walking through the narrow streets of Nazareth, one can still sense something of this darkness.

Yet God had chosen this very place as a home for His only begotten Son, the pure and sinless One, who left the glory of heaven to come to earth. How hard it must have been for the Boy Jesus to live among the children of Nazareth! And the mother Mary would have shared His distress. Parents suffer when their children are so different from other children that they are treated rather like strangers; when they have to go their way alone because no one really understands them.

So it would have been with the Boy Jesus, only to a far greater extent, for His heart was above with His heavenly Father, whom He loved more than all else. Perhaps He still had an inkling of what He used to have in heaven. If even among ordinary children there are those who have a great longing for heaven and are restrained from joining in evil and impure activities, being grieved by such things, then how hard it must have been for the Boy Jesus to grow up among bad, sinful children, especially since He loved each one dearly with a divine love.

Amid all these trials and hardships the mother Mary had to bring up her little Jesus. This was her task, her responsibility, as mother. But very often it would have been the other way round. The nature of her Child, so different from that of others, and the aura of holiness surrounding Him would have time and again filled her with reverence and she would have silently worshipped in her heart, saying, "This is the Son of God. Yes, this Child of mine truly is the Son of God."

Holy Scripture tells us that the Child Jesus increased in wisdom as well as in favour with God and man. Does this not seem to indicate that something of His uniqueness was noticed, just as a child prodigy, a musical genius, for instance, cannot remain hidden?

Yes, the grace of God was upon Him and the wisdom of God poured from His lips. How pleasant His disposition must have been, how gracious His words! For we hear that later when He was a grown Man even His fellow-townsmen were amazed at the beautiful words that came from His lips (Luke 4:22). The real nature of a person is often most pronounced in childhood, and during Jesus' childhood Mary was privileged as no one else to observe something of His real self as the Son of God, for after all, He was her Child; He had been placed in her charge. She was closest to Him. More than anyone else she was permitted to gaze into His eyes. No doubt, He told her much of what was on His heart, and she was privileged to hear the most words from His lips.

Ever anew she would have been struck by the incomprehensible grace that God had entrusted His only begotten Son to her, allowing Him to grow up as a Child in her home. Did ever a person on earth receive a greater gift from God than she did in having Jesus for a Child?

Now his parents went to Jerusalem every year at the feast of the Passover. And when he was twelve years old, they went up according to custom; and when the feast was ended, as they were returning, the boy Jesus stayed behind in Jerusalem.

His parents did not know it, but supposing him to be in the company they went a day's journey, and they sought him among their kinsfolk and acquaintances; and when they did not find him, they returned to Jerusalem, seeking him. After three days they found him in the temple, sitting among the teachers, listening to them and asking them questions; and all who heard him were amazed at his understanding and his answers.

And when they saw him they were astonished; and his mother said to him, "Son, why have you treated us so? Behold, your father and I have been looking for you anxiously."

And he said to them, "How is it that you sought me? Did you not know that I must be in my Father's house?" And they did not understand the saying which he spoke to them.

And he went down with them and came to Nazareth, and was obedient to them; and his mother kept all these things in her heart. And Jesus increased in wisdom and in stature, and in favour with God and man.

Luke 2:41-52

The years passed by and Jesus grew older, reaching the age of twelve. Then came the great day when He could accompany His parents to the Temple for the first time. What a special occasion that was in the life of a Jewish family when the parents set out for the Temple with their twelve-year-old son! Now he would be admitted into the Jewish congregation; his childhood years were over and he had entered youth. When a boy turned twelve, his parents saw their child beginning an important chapter in his life.

Would not Mary's heart have been brimming over with thanksgiving towards God as they went up to

Jerusalem? The last time she had been to the Temple with her Child was probably at the presentation. Afterwards she had to flee with Him into the wilderness, where death in many forms sought the life of her Child. But God protected Him. Now she was permitted to go with Him to the Temple, the House of God, of which the Psalmist sang in times past: "How lovely is your dwelling-place, O Lord Almighty! My soul yearns, even faints for the courts of the Lord; my heart and my flesh cry out for the living God. Even the sparrow has found a home...a place near your altar, O Lord Almighty, my King and my God" (Psalm 84:1-3 NIV).

Before going up to Jerusalem, the Boy Jesus, we can imagine, would have questioned His mother eagerly all about the Temple and how God manifested Himself there. Did He not also ask the scribes, the teachers of the Law, many questions in the Temple and discuss everything with them in great wisdom? Now the moment had actually come when the Boy Jesus would enter the Temple of God and behold the dwelling-place of the Most High. If the hearts of pious Jews were filled with joy and longing at the thought of visiting the Temple, then how much more so the heart of the Boy Jesus? What expectation, longing and deep joy would have gripped Him at the thought that now at last He would enter His Father's house and dwelling-place! For this was where Jesus belonged, and there alone.

In the company of their relatives and acquaintances His parents made with Him the long journey from Nazareth up to Jerusalem, where they would bring sacrifices to God and worship Him. During the busy feast days, the general commotion, and the many encounters, they may well have failed to notice what profound feelings stirred the depths of His heart as He now tarried in the Temple. For the Son of God, who had left heaven and the intimate presence of the Father, it must have been like touching at long last the outermost hem of His Father's garment when He attended the services in the sanctuary, where His Father was worshipped and where everything revolved around Him. From His remark afterwards to His mother, "Did you not know that I must be in my Father's house?" we can sense the cry of His heart to be left there where His Father had made His dwelling on earth. Having to live so far apart from His Father, He yearned to taste a little of His presence again.

The Boy Jesus would have felt like one whose soul is parched and whose all-consuming desire is to slake this thirst. Now the long-desired moment had come when the Boy Jesus would taste the bliss of reunion. Scarcely able to restrain the surging joy, He would have said in His heart, "I shall never go away again. Here I shall stay, for this is My home."

Just how much He must have been longing for the Father all the time is evident from the way He felt at home in the House of God. Even though the sons of men, as He later said, had turned it into a den of thieves, He found there His Father's dwelling and would have preferred to stay there. As a mother loves her child and joyfully takes him into her arms upon finding him again, even if he bears the traces of a sinful life, so in spite of the distortion of God's dwelling-place the Son found the Father in the Temple.

Could not Mary, the mother of Jesus, have sensed what was going on in her Son's mind? To all pious Jews the Temple meant a great deal; for them, as no doubt for Mary, it was the dwelling-place of God.

Could she not have foreseen that in the Temple her Child, the Son of God, would feel at home and spend such happy days there that it would be hard for Him to go away? Even if she may have pondered this in her heart beforehand, the reality of everyday life proved to be too strong.

It was customary to return after the feast, and because Mary had never experienced anything but absolute obedience from her Child, it did not occur to her that her Son would not follow them in the company of the other pilgrims on their homeward journey when the festivities were over. How great was the parents' dismay when they did not find Him at the place where they lodged for the night and no one knew of His whereabouts!

Who, then, can fail to understand the mother Mary's question to her Son when she found Him at last? — "Son, why have you treated us so? Behold, your father and I have been looking for you anxiously." We all know what it is like for parents when their child is missing. Anxiously they search for him, their apprehension growing from hour to hour lest something has happened to him and they have lost him for ever. Only because Mary loved her Son so dearly, could her grief be so great when she did not find Him and had perhaps already given Him up for lost.

She found Him in the Temple among the teachers of the Law, listening and asking questions. After all the anguish her heart had endured because of Him, she could hardly take it in that her Child had now been returned to her. However, it was not the pure joy of reunion. In Luke 2:48 it says, "When they saw him they were astonished." On this occasion the mother Mary experienced in a more concrete form than ever before that her Son Jesus was uniquely different from everyone else and lived in another sphere. She heard the replies He gave the scribes; she saw their amazement; and she herself marvelled at the divine wisdom in His words. She realized that He was no longer the Child she knew from back home, even though He had always been endowed with divine graces.

For Mary the divinely appointed day had come when God made it very clear to her: "Your Child is no longer yours." This is why God probably so arranged it that after those hours of great anxiety, when her mother-love was aroused more than ever, she had that experience. It left an indelible impression upon her soul, especially after the anguish she had undergone. There in the Temple of God, Jesus sat among the teachers of the Law as if He belonged there and as if this were His rightful place. And the reply that now came from the lips of her Child, "Did you not know that I must be in My Father's house?" was meant to be God's answer to her question. Yes, He had to be there. This is where He belonged. And this He demonstrated to her by His course of action.

Thus even as a twelve-year-old, Jesus drew the dividing line between His parents and Himself with His reply: Not Joseph, but God, was His father. And just as in the first years Mary had especially to learn to have faith, so now she had to learn to detach herself from her Son. He was taken from her. The sword began to pierce her heart and with every year more so till her Son hung on the cross. There the dividing line was drawn for good when Jesus said, though with caring, filial love, "Woman, behold, your son — John!"

Are we now surprised that Scripture when describing the incident with the twelve-year-old Jesus in the

Temple says of His parents, "They did not understand the saying which he spoke to them"? Sensing from Jesus' words the absoluteness of His affiliation to God the Father, they were filled with such grief at Jesus' dissociation from them, His parents, that all knowledge and understanding of His destiny was drowned in this anguish. They could sense that there was more to it than a pious Jewish child feeling drawn to the House of the Lord; and this "more", which only the divinity of Jesus could account for, caused them such deep sorrow as parents that it was impossible for them to understand Him at that moment.

Even if Mary's Son had been restored to her, He had actually been taken from her, for God the Father had clearly demonstrated to her in the Temple episode, "This Child is Mine, My only begotten Son; He belongs to Me, and Me alone." To be sure, Jesus returned with His parents to Nazareth as an obedient Son and was once again subject to them in everything. But a threshold had been crossed, even though everything was back to normal.

Mary, however — the Bible says explicitly — treasured all these words in her heart. She did not ignore them but pondered on them, as we hear of her each time. Had she dismissed them, she might have been tempted to think that nothing had changed as she saw her Son submitting to her in everyday life and fitting in with the routine of family life like any other child. But she refused to go by appearances. The words she had heard from His lips abided with her as the greater reality. Unable to forget them, she contemplated them in her heart.

In so doing, she demonstrated that although she did not understand Him she did in a sense. By taking His words seriously, she expressed a willingness to

79

understand Him and to be obedient to God.

Thus she was the first to pay the price of discipleship, learning and practising what Jesus would later say to all His disciples as a challenge and as a condition to following Him: "If any one comes to me and does not hate his own father and mother and wife and children and brothers and sisters...he cannot be my disciple" (Luke 14:26). Following God's leadings means detaching ourselves from others, including those closest to us. Jesus Himself forsook the Father for our sakes; and now Mary too had to tread the path of forsaking — as would later all His disciples — and let go of Him as her Child. No doubt, in the following years she could sense more and more that He was being taken away from her: He lived in a completely different world and the heavenly Father was His great love.

But in addition to this grief, which she had to endure in all its bitterness as mother, inner conflict would have assailed her increasingly as time went on. "If He is the Son of God and about His Father's business, why does He not reveal Himself as the Son of God? Why does He not bear witness to the Father? Why does He not ascend the throne of David as king and why has He not become a light for the Gentiles, as was promised? He is not even a light for Israel, for you do not hide a light under a bushel."

Yet His divine gifts, which she and others had already noticed, were truly placed under a bushel. He lived as a simple son of a carpenter, presumably following His father's trade, year in year out fashioning doors, wooden ploughs, and other tools for the Nazarenes. Was not David taken away from his lowly occupation as shepherd to be anointed king while still a lad? Why did none of the priests and Pharisees ask after her Son?

In a new and deeper way the mother Mary had to learn to keep faith and wait patiently for God's timing. At first she would have waited from one year to the next, and then, when Jesus entered manhood, from month to month, week to week, and finally from day to day, for the moment when at last He would disclose His identity and when the angel's prophecy at the annunciation of His birth would be fulfilled. Would God now give Him the throne of His father David? Would He be proclaimed king of Israel and enter upon His God-given office and calling?

But there was not the slightest indication in this direction. Since Jesus belonged to the lowly family of a carpenter in Nazareth, He had no connections whatsoever with influential groups, let alone with the ruling class of Israel. How often would the mother Mary have raised the question when she came before God in prayer: "Where is the fulfilment of the promise, O Lord? When will it come?" And when she was disappointed every day anew, she had to battle through in prayer every day anew to lay hold of the promise again in faith; and so her faith actually consisted of innumerable acts of faith and dedication to God.

A comparison can be drawn to Abraham. In spite of the promise he had received, he was confronted ever anew with the barrenness of Sarah, who bore him no son. Similarly, Mary watched her Son grow up — in those times a thirteen-year-old boy in Israel was already considered an adult and capable of starting a career — and still He made no step towards the fulfilment of the promise. How often she would have said, "My Lord and God, I do not understand You!" But just as she once expressed with her "Let it be to me", so she would have battled through ever anew

81

until she reached the point where she could believe again and say in faith, "But I trust You, and the day is coming when in spite of everything You will place Him on the throne of David so that He might save His people!"

7

Mary During the First Stage of Jesus' Public Ministry

On the third day a wedding took place at Cana in Galilee. Jesus' mother was there, and Jesus and his disciples had also been invited to the wedding. When the wine was gone, Jesus' mother said to him, "They have no more wine."

"Dear woman, why do you involve me?" Jesus replied, "My time has not yet come."

His mother said to the servants, "Do whatever he tells you."

Nearby stood six stone water jars, the kind used by the Jews for ceremonial washing, each holding from twenty to thirty gallons. Jesus said to the servants, "Fill the jars with water"; so they filled them to the brim. Then he told them, "Now draw some out and take it to the master of the banquet."

They did so, and the master of the banquet tasted the water that had been turned into wine. He did not realize where it had come from, though the servants who had drawn the water knew. Then he called the bridegroom aside and said, "Everyone brings out the choice wine first and then the cheaper wine after the guests have had too much to drink; but you have saved the best till now."

This, the first of his miraculous signs, Jesus performed in Cana of Galilee. He thus revealed his glory, and his disciples put their faith in him. After this he went down to Capernaum.

John 2:1-12 NIV

He who waits can sense when that which he has awaited is drawing nigh and his hopes are about to materialize. So it was with the mother Mary at the wedding feast at Cana. In the meantime Jesus had gathered around Him disciples, and that would have been like a ray of hope for her. His life had taken a new direction. Quite likely she hoped that now the moment had come when God would fulfil His promises at last and her Son would ascend the throne of David. For so long she had waited yearningly for this to happen. Had the time now come for Him to perform His first public miracle and thus demonstrate to all the people that He was the Christ?

Believing in her Son's power, Mary had complete confidence in His ability to handle every situation. This is why during the wedding festivities when the wine ran out and this situation of need arose, she immediately turned to Jesus, saying, "They have no wine", as if it were perfectly natural to look to Him to provide a solution and replenish the wine. Jesus' answer to her, sometimes rendered as, "O woman, what have you to do with me?" is usually misinterpreted. Literally it means, "What to me and to you?" (a Semitic formula), and does not have an unfriendly tone as it does in English.

Jesus went on to say, "My hour has not yet come." From this we see that He had understood His mother even though He would not let her press Him. With this reply He probably also wanted to say to her, "The hour is certainly coming when I shall reveal My power and bring help, but it has not yet arrived and I have to wait in obedience till the Father shows Me when to act."

"My hour has not yet come..." No doubt for many years, day after day, God had been teaching Mary to accept precisely this. Once again, she humbly accepted this word, at the same time believing in the mission of her Son, as is evident from her instruction to the servants, "Do whatever He tells you." On that day His hour really had come, only a little later than Mary had hoped. The first great miracle took place at this wedding, and it is written that Jesus thereby manifested His glory.

Whose heart would have been filled with greater joy and adoration than that of His mother Mary! Of the disciples it is written that they put their faith in Him. But Mary had long since done so. This is why she wished to encourage Him with her request to perform the miracle. After all those years of waiting, hoping against hope, and then being disappointed, after battling through in faith ever anew, walking on in patience, trusting that His hour would still come — what must it have meant for Mary that now a public miracle had taken place! For the first time Jesus had displayed His greatness and His power for all to see.

Her thanksgiving to God would have been boundless now that He began to fulfil His promises. Something of His glory had become visible through her Son, who had proved His miraculous power as the Son of God. Though so far no way had opened up for Jesus to ascend the throne of David, this could still be the beginning of the path that would lead there — now that it became increasingly known among His people what divine power He possessed. In this hope she would have let Him go when He left His parental home in Nazareth to take up residence in Capernaum with His disciples.

This marked a great change in the life of the mother Mary. For thirty years she had had the privilege of living under one roof with her Child, who was the Son of God and from whom the glory of God shone forth time and again. As His mother and confidante she had had a deep and loving relationship with Him, as is natural for a proper mother and her son. And now she had to detach herself completely from Him, a process that had begun in Jesus' twelfth year when God first drew the dividing line in her soul.

Jesus returned to Galilee in the power of the Spirit, and news about him spread through the whole countryside. He taught in their synagogues, and everyone praised him.

He went to Nazareth, where he had been brought up, and on the Sabbath day he went into the synagogue, as was his custom. And he stood up to read. The scroll of the prophet Isaiah was handed to him. Unrolling it, he found the place where it is written: "The Spirit of the Lord is on me, because he has anointed me to preach good news to the poor. He has sent me to proclaim freedom for the prisoners and recovery of sight for the blind, to release the oppressed, to proclaim the year of the Lord's favour."

Then he rolled up the scroll, gave it back to the attendant and sat down. The eyes of everyone in the synagogue were fastened on him, and he began by saying to them, "Today this scripture is fulfilled in your hearing." All spoke well of him and were amazed at the gracious words that came from his lips. "Isn't this Joseph's son?" they asked.

Jesus said to them, "Surely you will quote this proverb to me: 'Physician, heal yourself! Do here in your home town what we have heard that you did in Capernaum.'"

"I tell you the truth," he continued, "no prophet is accepted in his home town. I assure you that there were many widows in Israel in Elijah's time, when the sky was shut for three and a half years and there was a severe famine throughout the land. Yet Elijah was not sent to any of them, but to a widow in Zarephath in the region of Sidon. And there were many in Israel with leprosy in the time of Elisha the prophet, yet not one of them was cleansed — only Naaman the Syrian."

All the people in the synagogue were furious when they heard this. They got up, drove him out of the town, and

took him to the brow of the hill on which the town was
built, in order to throw him down the cliff. But he walked
right through the crowd and went on his way.

Luke 4:14-30 NIV

Did ever a person experience such a crushing blow
to his hopes and expectations as the mother Mary did
shortly after Jesus had entered upon His public
ministry? To be sure, in the first weeks after He had
left Nazareth she heard that He was performing
many mighty deeds, that the fame of Him was
spreading throughout Judea and Galilee, and that
people were flocking to Him, drawn by the great and
wonderful healings. At the wedding in Cana the
mother Mary showed how much she had been waiting
for the revelation of His power and glory, and so
these recent developments would have filled her with
deep joy. Not only as a mother but as the recipient of
God's promise concerning Jesus, she would have rejoiced that what He had said was coming true. At last
Jesus was beginning to manifest Himself in His mission as Saviour of His people.

And then He came to His home town Nazareth.
Surely a different welcome would await Him compared to all the other times He returned, perhaps
after doing a job out of town. Surely His townsfolk
would receive Him with great expectation and gladness, at last honouring Him instead of contemptuously seeing in Him the mere son of a carpenter. How
the mother Mary would have set her hopes on His
coming, for the news of her Son's mighty deeds
would certainly have reached Nazareth too!

It was a great day for Nazareth, but also for His
mother, when Jesus spoke in the synagogue to His
townsfolk. Perhaps for the first time Mary heard Him

deliver the Word publicly. The divine wisdom of Jesus, which had shone forth from Him, though half-veiled, during His conversation with the teachers of the Law in the Temple, was now to become visible to all, this time coming from the lips of the mature Man. It was to become manifest that the Spirit of God dwelt in Him, yes, that He was now speaking to His townsfolk as the Son of God.

Would Mary have already envisioned Him speaking to the vast throngs in the Temple the next time He went up to Jerusalem, with the teachers of the Law once again listening reverently and then perhaps anointing Him king? Surely now everyone would recognize in Him the Son of God. Surely now the time had come at last when He would ascend the throne of David, and the angel's prophecy would be fulfilled: He would come to His people as the Messiah in order to save them.

It was probably seldom that the synagogue in Nazareth was so full as on that occasion when Jesus, a son of the town, about whom so many wonderful reports were circulating, began to speak. And it was probably seldom that the people listened with such rapt attention as on that day, for as Scripture says, "The eyes of all in the synagogue were fixed on him" (Luke 4:20). They all heard the powerful words that came from His lips — words so gracious that they marvelled at them. But did they now humbly honour Him? Did they exclaim, "Truly, this is the Son of God, our Messiah!" And did they confess with shame, "How could we have failed to recognize Him before, treating Him unworthily and doing Him wrong?" For such unkind acts could have happened all too easily in a small place like Nazareth, where everyone lived at close quarters.

But no, this was not the response of their hearts. They did not declare, "Is not this the Messiah, the Son of God?" Instead they said, "Is not this Joseph's son?" By their attitude they showed that they did not accept Him as the Messiah or king of Israel. To the King of kings one can only submit; to the Messiah, Saviour and Redeemer, one can only surrender oneself in body, soul, and spirit. This is what the mother Mary would have been waiting for in that hour.

Apart from a few voices expressing admiration, we may assume that in all those years in Nazareth the mother Mary had heard many voices calling her Son peculiar because He was not like others. No doubt, He was subject to much criticism and cold-shouldering, as it invariably is with a person whom others do not understand because he is different from them, greater than them. He is ignored by his fellow beings, rejected or even tormented by those who envy him. They seek to degrade him, because they feel humiliated by the difference they can sense between him and them.

For Mary's mother-heart how agonizing it was to experience the rejection of her Son on the day of His revelation in His home town! What grieved her most of all was that her Son was rejected here as the Son of God, and not just by anybody but by their kinsfolk and many acquaintances, at whose houses they were frequent visitors and whom they knew from childhood.

It is impossible to remain neutral in our relationship to the Messiah and Son of God. Thus Jesus' first public appearance in His home town and disclosure of His identity immediately resulted in division — in rejection, yes, anger and fierce hatred. Although He was one of them, having grown up in their midst, and although wonderful reports about Him had reached them from all sides, they thrust Him out of the town. Taking Him to the edge of the hill on which their town was built, they, unbelievably, sought to push Him headlong over the cliff.

The people of His home town were the first to threaten Him with death and make an attempt on His life. Would not the sword have wounded the heart of the mother Mary, yes, piercing it deeply? It could not be otherwise, for she witnessed it all. She heard the angry words and outbursts of hatred, saw with terror how they led Him to the hilltop, and went through agonies as they attempted to hurl her Son down. His deliverance was nothing less than a miracle of divine intervention.

Messiah, king of Israel, installed on the throne of David? Now her hopes lay dashed before her. How incomprehensible God's leadings must have seemed to her! Can we imagine how hard it must have been for the mother Mary to go on living in Nazareth? She had lost her Son doubly, for after that assault on His life He would hardly ever return to Nazareth and she would see Him but rarely. Moreover, she lived among those who hated her Son and day after day, or so we may assume, she had to listen to them reviling Him. Once again, she came under disgrace as mother of this Jesus.

* Regarded by some in its wider sense: cousins, relations.

How much difficulty the relatives would have caused her, for we read in John 7 that the brothers* of Jesus did not believe in Him either, perhaps out of envy like the brothers of the patriarch Joseph, whose trials prefigured those of Christ. As the feast of Tabernacles drew near, they criticized and reproached Him, saying, "Leave here and go to Judea, that your disciples may see the works you are doing. For no man works in secret if he seeks to be known openly. If you do these things, show yourself to the world" (John 7:3f.). And then we read on, "For even his brothers did not believe in him." Yet these very brothers had seen Him making a public appearance in the synagogue at Nazareth and ministering openly. But whatever Jesus did, they were annoyed and furious with Him and made His life a misery.

They would have also made the life of His mother a misery, for they could probably sense how attached the mother's heart was to this Son and that she believed in Him. He was the promised Child, the Son of God, this Son of hers — Jesus.

Then Jesus entered a house, and again a crowd gathered, so that he and his disciples were not even able to eat. When his family heard about this, they went to take charge of him, for they said, "He is out of his mind."

Mark 3:20f. NIV

Then Jesus' mother and brothers arrived. Standing outside, they sent someone in to call him. A crowd was sitting around him, and they told him, "Your mother and brothers are outside looking for you."

"Who are my mother and my brothers?" he asked. Then

he looked at those seated in a circle around him and said, "Here are my mother and my brothers! Whoever does God's will is my brother and sister and mother."

Mark 3:31-35 NIV

Presumably the Bible was referring to Jesus' brothers when it says that His family set out to take charge of Him and declared that He was out of His mind, for in the same chapter we read that His nearest relations came to Him. This time mention is made of His mother, who together with His brothers asked for Him. Does not the verdict of His relatives, "He is out of his mind!" reflect the condemning attitude of His home town, of all those who had heard Him in the synagogue? Having once rejected Him, they had to justify their hostility towards Him. Perhaps they accused Him of being an idler, living off alms and the possessions of women. He ought to be about His work, they would have objected, instead of wandering through the country as a miracle worker and causing a commotion everywhere.

All this would have filled the mother Mary with much distress and she would have longed to speak with her Son. We are not told what the mother Mary wanted to say to Him. Perhaps she merely wished to see Him again and pour out her heart with its many Why's about this pathway, which did not seem to lead to the fulfilment of the promise. Besides, she was greatly concerned for the life of her Son. She would certainly have heard of the plots and schemes of the Pharisees, which are mentioned earlier on in this chapter (Mark 3:6). Perhaps it was on her heart to suggest to Him that He remain more in seclusion now that His life was at stake. On the other hand, the people pressed Him so hard that He was not even able to eat and drink, and this too would have aroused her concern. And who knows what else may have been troubling her mind? As a frail human being born of our sinful humanity and subject to temptation, she would have been unable to understand her Son's actions. And all the gossip of the Nazarenes would have increased her doubts. This is probably why she rushed to Him and sought to speak with Him.

Upon hearing that His relatives were asking for Him, Jesus said, "Whoever does the will of God is my brother, and sister, and mother", thus drawing even more sharply the dividing line first indicated by His conduct as a twelve-year-old in the Temple. Jesus did not come to Mary as she requested. He did not come although she was longing to see Him and speak to Him. She had to let go of Him, severing the bonds of human motherhood and releasing Him for His great, divine mission.

Some take these verses from the Gospel of Mark to mean that the only relationship Mary had to Jesus was on a human level — that of a mother. But considering that Mary had to go through the painful process of letting go of her Son and severing human ties, was this not a sign that she had been called to follow Jesus on a spiritual level as His disciple? And if none of Jesus' kinsfolk could understand His leading and even John the Baptist began to have doubts, then surely Mary would not have been spared inner conflict either as she observed the direction her Son's life had taken? Her faith could be genuine only if it had been tried and tested in the crucible of doubts and temptations. This does not in any way detract from what Scripture says of the mother Mary: "Blessed is she who believed." The fact that she suffered so much anguish and inner conflict makes her walk with the Lord all the more credible.

Jesus' reply, given publicly, was a new milestone on her path of discipleship. Humbled in the presence of all the people, she had to accept that she was no longer His mother according to the flesh but only through the Spirit of God if she obeyed the Son. A great change became evident in her relationship to Jesus. Once Jesus had to be subject to her as His mother; now she had to be subject to Him and do the will of God, as He made it known to her. Only then could she continue to belong to Him.

Would not these words of His have pierced the heart of the mother Mary like a sword? For here Jesus chose other mothers and brothers, not on a human level but on a spiritual level — those who were doers of His will. In that painful moment did Mary think of Simeon's prophecy about the sword and did she say again, "Let it be to me according to your word"? Since her life was characterized by this saying, she would have battled through again to an obedient "Let it be to me" and thus proved herself to be the humble handmaid of the Lord, whose lowliness He had regarded. This is why she could also be mother of Jesus in the spiritual sense, for doing His will is the salient feature of one called to be His mother.

If on the one hand Mary had to die to her old self at the message that everyone who does the will of God may be Jesus' mother, on the other hand she was the first to receive the glad tidings that are now meant for us all: everyone who lives in the obedience of faith is privileged to bring Jesus to the world as His mother was, privileged to be a brother and sister to Him, privileged to belong to Him completely and to share everything with Him. As on another occasion, recorded in Luke 11, when in reply to a woman's enthusiastic cry Jesus said, "Blessed rather are those who hear the word of God and keep it!" here too Jesus demonstrated how precious spiritual motherhood is. And this motherhood Mary retained, for frequent mention is made of her keeping His words.

8
Mary Accompanies
Her Son to the Cross

From that time Jesus began to show to his disciples that he must go to Jerusalem, and suffer many things from the elders and chief priests and scribes, and be killed, and be raised again the third day.

Then Peter took him aside and began to rebuke him, saying, "Far be it from you, Lord; this shall not happen to you!" But he turned and said to Peter, "Get behind me, Satan! You are an offence to me, for you are not mindful of the things of God, but the things of men."

Matthew 16:21-23 RAV

Of all those who loved Jesus and accompanied Him as His followers during the three years of His public ministry, how many suspected that His death was so imminent? To be sure, His disciples were conscious of the great antagonism of the Pharisees, time and again witnessing how they sought to kill Jesus. But Mary, who with a mother's sympathy and intuition was quick to take in everything pertaining to her Son, would not only have heard that His life was threatened, this being common knowledge: the dangers that He faced would have weighed continually on her heart.

We know what the disciples' reaction was when Jesus spoke to them plainly about His Passion and death. They did not take it in. They did not understand the saying, as we read in Scripture. They did not consider it true or remotely possible that He would suffer. Even a man like Peter said, "This shall never happen to You!" In retrospect we ask how he could speak like that and try to evade suffering. But considering the circumstances in which he said this, it is understandable. Peter was the one who had believed and declared Jesus to be the Son of God. And Jesus Himself had repeatedly said that He was eternal Life. How, then, could God be killed by men? Eternal life is immortal.

Would the mother Mary have thought any differently? Even before the birth of Jesus it was made known to her supernaturally that the Child she would give birth to was the Son of God. And had she not experienced many miraculous instances of protection beginning with the massacre of the innocents and the flight to Egypt? Later when His fellow-countrymen in Nazareth sought to push Him over the cliff, He passed through their midst and went His way sovereignly. Death could not touch Him. Moreover, she had received from the lips of the angel the very special promise that her Son would ascend the throne of David. She must have firmly expected this promise to come true, for the other promise had also come true: namely, that the Holy Spirit would come upon her and she would conceive by the power of the Spirit of God.

Was she not obliged to cling to the angel's promise, especially seeing that she had taken it seriously? Was she at all permitted to think, assume or believe that Jesus would now die an untimely death at the age of thirty-three, His work still unfinished? For her that would have been unbelief and disobedience towards God. She could not have understood, as indeed none of the disciples could — not even when Jesus ascended to heaven – that He would not establish His kingdom in Israel during His lifetime, or after His resurrection, or through the miracle of Pentecost (Acts 1:3,6). Not until some two thousand years later when Jesus comes again, is received by His people as Messiah, establishes His reign in Israel and ascends the throne of David, will the promise concerning His everlasting kingdom reach its ultimate fulfilment. But all this was still a mystery hidden from the eyes of the disciples.

Everything would have seemed more and more meaningless to Mary as Holy Week drew near and Jesus prepared to tread His path of sorrows, which would end in torment and death. God had so ordained it that this last phase of suffering, culminating in the crucifixion, came just before the Passover. We heard how Joseph and Mary went up to Jerusalem yearly to celebrate the feast. Consequently, Mary happened to be in the city during those days and inevitably experienced it all. Truly, what she endured was far more than a mother watching her child die a horrible death. She suffered not only as a mother in the flesh when she shared in the pain of her Son. She suffered primarily on a spiritual level, just as Abraham suffered when he led his son to the place of sacrifice.

How greatly Abraham suffered when he was called to offer up his own child and deal him the deathblow himself! But for him the greatest anguish was having to bury a promise of God. It seemed as though God were contradicting Himself. As a chosen one of the Lord, who bore within him the divine promises, he held the counsels and purposes of God in high regard. Indeed, he was to be instrumental in carrying them out. This is why the sacrifice required of him touched him at his most sensitive spot. He was therefore in danger of losing confidence in God, and his faith may well have threatened to crumble to pieces. For is it not true, we are able to bear the greatest sufferings if we are resting in the will of God, knowing that on these pathways He is leading us to glory? But paths of suffering become hard and unbearable if they are fraught with trials and temptations because we can no longer understand God, who seems to be acting contrary to His promises.

This was the inner turmoil that the mother Mary found herself in when the news of her Son's arrest reached her. She would scarcely have been able to believe it. Instead of passing sovereignly through the midst of His captors and demonstrating His divine power, as He had done back then in Nazareth, He allowed His hands to be bound by a small group of soldiers, submitting to them like a weak and helpless human being. In the triumphal procession of His foes, He was then dragged to the Sanhedrin to stand trial before the very men who had long sought to kill Him.

How distressing it must have been for the pious heart of Mary that the religious leaders of the people, those whom she regarded as God's representatives on earth, took proceedings against her Son in the name of God and that God did not take His side although this was His Son! Could not Jesus have convinced the scribes and Pharisees with His words, as once long ago as a twelve-year-old in the Temple? Could He not have demonstrated to them with mighty deeds that He — and not they — had been commissioned by God? Like the disciple Peter, Mary would time and again have been in the vicinity of the High Priest's palace in order to be near Jesus and to hear the latest developments, never giving up hope that Jesus would still prove who He was.

Right up to the last moment the disciples too had probably hoped and expected that Jesus would prove Himself as the Son of God, who does miracles, and as the king of Israel. Perhaps it was their secret hope that precisely when the Sanhedrin and the people sought to condemn Him to death, He would manifest Himself as the One who alone has power over them and before whom they must all bow down. But then Mary had to hear that Annas and Caiaphas had declared her Son guilty of death, and her hopes sank.

But one glimmer of hope still remained. Only if the procurator Pilate gave his assent could Jesus actually be put to death. Was it not reasonable to suppose that Pilate would refuse to ratify the death sentence? As a Roman he would surely have no interest in ordering the execution of a Jewish man who could not be accused of any crime? Filled with trepidation, the mother Mary may have stood among the crowds in the courtyard at the Fortress of Antonia and listened from afar as to how the trial against Jesus was continuing. How her heart would have ached, nearly crushed by the burden of grief and sorrow when she saw her Son exposed to hatred far greater than what He had faced back then in Nazareth, when His townsfolk had tried to kill Him! She must have been cut to the quick to hear her own people, incited by the Pharisees, utter those terrible, hate-filled words to Pilate, "Crucify him, crucify him! Away with this man!"

What untold disgrace for her that her Son, who was given to her as the Son of God, was considered a criminal, unfit to live on this earth! What immeasurable anguish for her that He reaped nothing but hatred for all the love and kindness He had sown those years among His people! And what a grief for her as a frail woman to watch on powerless! Not a single one of all the men who owed their lives to Him, not one of His disciples spoke up on His behalf. No crowd now arose to bear witness to Him and make an effort to save His life.

With their rejection and hatred of her Son, the people repudiated the Holy One in Him, God Himself, and that would have grieved Mary even more deeply. Although many aspects of His divine sonship were a mystery to her, few knew better than she that He was indeed the Holy One. And then there was the agonizing cry welling up in her heart: "It cannot be that He will be slain. Did not God say in His message that His Son is eternal Life and that He will become the king of Israel?" The sword that Simeon had prophesied for her pierced her many times over, sinking deeper and deeper into her heart.

Jesus' path of sorrows, instead of ending immediately in death upon His arrest, consisted of many stages: the four trials, the mockery, then the scourging and crowning with thorns. As Mary accompanied her Son to the cross, she shared in spirit the pain of each step along that path.

She would certainly have heard of His scourging and the cruel suffering involved. We do not know whether she could actually see her Son as He stood, covered with blood, at the whipping post in the courtyard at Pilate's palace. And if she did, she would no doubt have turned her eyes away, unable to bear the sight. It would have torn her heart to hear the swish of the lashes upon His body. Once she had been privileged to care for this body in His childhood years, and as she did so, she would have doubtless sensed something of the mystery of God being manifest in the flesh. She knew what agonizing pain the iron barbs of the lashes caused as they pierced the flesh, ripping out whole chunks. From reports of the punishment inflicted upon criminals, she would have also been aware of how close the victims came to death. Now when her own Son stood there in a pool of blood she could do nothing. There was absolutely no way she could help Him. All she could do was let the sword bore deeper into her heart at every step further along His way of sorrows.

Nor would she have been spared the sight of her Son publicly exposed to utmost shame and degradation. To all the people who had assembled in Jerusalem for the feast, Jesus was presented wearing a crown of thorns and a fool's garment. He was disfigured beyond recognition, His face bruised and swollen from the lashes of the whip and the strokes of the rod, His garment stained with the spittle of those who spat upon Him. And from the thorns piercing His brow, blood trickled down continually upon His face. This is the state in which she now had to see her Son, who according to the promise she had received was destined to wear the crown of the king of Israel. In that moment the last ray of hope in her probably flickered out and she could only pray fervently, "Lord, have mercy! Lord, have mercy!" The suffering was so abysmal that it was almost more than a human heart could bear.

Yet the suffering of our Lord Jesus was not over. He was to endure the full measure of suffering for us, so as to obtain the fullness of glory for us. Thus He was spared nothing, not even the cruel death on the cross. God led His plan of salvation to its goal. Corresponding to the extent of our sin and guilt, Jesus had to drain the cup of suffering and then on the cross to crush the head of the serpent. Only by becoming a curse for us on the cross — as Scripture says, "Cursed be every one who hangs on a tree" (Galatians 3:13) — could He redeem us.

In sharing the path of her Son, the mother Mary was not spared any affliction. Seldom, if ever, did a mother suffer with her child such an abundance of physical pain and torment or such anguish of soul. Her spirit too was rent with suffering, harrowed by trials and temptations, because she could no longer understand God's leadings, and the agony of unfulfilled promises was almost unbearable.

Then Jesus had to carry His heavy cross to Calvary. Perhaps the scribes led the way, arranging for a trumpeter to announce which criminal was being led to the place of execution. The rabble followed in large numbers, hooting and jeering as they went. In the narrow streets of Jerusalem not only taunts reached Him, but people may have thrown objects at Him from the balconies and spat at Him. For we know that the people were carried away with hatred and fury. And it is very likely, as old traditions say, that Jesus broke down a number of times under the burden of the cross, having already been tortured to the point of death.

The mother Mary would have mingled with the crowd or stood in one of the side streets to catch a glimpse of Him as He swayed through the streets beneath the heavy cross, amid the jeers of the mob. It is not far-fetched to suppose that she too came under scorn and ridicule. Was not Peter immediately recognized as one of those who were with Jesus and pointed at contemptuously? So it may well have been with the mother of Jesus. God alone knows what she suffered. But He gathers our tears in a bottle (Psalm 56:8) and will place them as pearls in our crown one day above, for according to our suffering, so will our glory be.

The procession reached the hill of Golgotha. Her Son was deprived of His clothes and stood naked before all the people. Then He was laid on the wooden beam of the cross, and the terrible moment came for the mother Mary when she heard the hammer blows as the huge nails were driven into His flesh. In former times she had often heard the sound of hammering in her house when Joseph and Jesus too drove nails into wood. But this time — oh, how incomprehensible it must have been for her! — the hammer pounded on nails piercing the hands and feet of her own Son. Would not cries of horror have come from her lips at the gruesome treatment her Son was made to suffer?

And God was silent. He was silent and permitted all this to happen. What immeasurable anguish she must have suffered in her soul! She had to look on while her Son suffered excruciating pain, for crucifixion is known to be the most agonizing of all deaths. The victims often went out of their minds and are said to have bellowed like bulls. But Jesus suffered like a lamb. Perhaps all one heard from His lips was a gentle moaning. He endured the torments in all their intensity, drinking the cup of suffering to its last bitter drop, and with Him His mother, who stood beneath the cross. All the disciples, apart from John, had fled. But not so His mother. She remained with Jesus in order to share His suffering. What greater proof could there be of genuine discipleship?

Standing by the cross of Jesus were his mother, and his mother's sister, Mary the wife of Clopas, and Mary Magdalene.

105

When Jesus saw his mother, and the disciple whom he loved standing near, he said to his mother, "Woman, behold, your son!" Then he said to the disciple, "Behold, your mother!" And from that hour the disciple took her to his own home.

John 19:25-27

Upon whom did Jesus' gaze fall during the inexpressible agony of His last hours? Upon Mary, His mother. He who was in need of comfort as never before and would soon cry out, "My God, my God, why hast thou forsaken me?" did not want His mother to feel forsaken in her deep grief when He now went from her. Jesus knew what she had to endure, even if we tend to forget it or are often disinclined to acknowledge it. This is why He now had a word for her: "Woman, behold, your son!"

Words uttered in such an agonizing hour of death are of special significance. They hold good. The words that now came from Jesus' lips showed what was most alive in His soul: a forgiving love towards all people, the triumphant assurance of having accomplished His work, and the surrender of His will with the committal of His Spirit into the hands of the Father. In that hour He tasted the depths of agony and God-forsakenness, but at the same time His heart overflowed with compassion and tender, caring love for His mother and for the disciple closest to Him. Yes, those who loved Him the most and those who suffered the most because of Him, to them He granted, as people often do in their dying hour, His last glance and last word.

And Jesus said to His mother, "Behold, your son — John is now your son." How much lies hidden in these words! Why did Jesus give John to the mother

Mary as a son? It was God speaking to her in the Person of Jesus. God gives when He takes. This is a divine law. Jesus knew how much it would cost the mother Mary when the Father now took Him away from her. This could not be compared to a mother losing her son, however great the pain may be of losing a son in the prime of his life. There was no bereavement like hers, for according to God's promise her Son should not have been taken away before she had experienced the fulfilment of the promise: the establishment of His kingdom. Indeed, death should never have been able to touch Him, since He was the Son of God.

Knowing that her grief would be immeasurably great, Jesus singled her out for the divine comfort of being entrusted with a son, a spiritual son. He gave her the one who had loved Him the most and had understood Him best in His divine sonship and His divine mission and in whom Jesus would now come closest to her. In him she received Jesus' true legacy, for John, His favourite disciple, had been very close to His heart. Now she was to spend the rest of her life with him.

And what must it have meant for John that Jesus then said, "Behold, your mother!" With that, He wished to give John too a special consolation, for John's grief at his Master coming to such a tragic end no doubt exceeded that of all the other disciples. Thus Jesus granted him the great consolation of sharing his home from that time onwards with His mother, the woman who had been closest to Him. Even before the birth of Jesus she had been instructed by God about Him and from the very first day of His life she shared in His sorrows and hardships and everything else. Yes, Jesus wanted to bring John into a close relationship with His mother so that John would always have something of Jesus with him.

With these words of His on the cross Jesus lovingly provided for His mother and the disciple John. It was a foretaste of divine recompense for their immeasurable suffering and their loss of Jesus through this gruesome crucifixion. Was Mary capable of taking in the consolation that the love of Jesus offered her as she stood beneath the cross? It would doubtless have also been like a stab of the sword and a deep grief for her that Jesus should now give her His disciple as a son in exchange for Himself. But one thing would most assuredly have been a comfort to her and that was to receive a personal word from the lips of her Son, the Son of God, a word expressive of Jesus' great love for her and showing how much He thought of her and cared for her. And so she was privileged to go on being mother — if not to Him, then to the one who had been so close to Him, to His disciple John and no doubt to many others.

Later when our Lord Jesus had ascended to heaven and she had made her home with John, she would have thanked Jesus ever anew for giving her this consolation and task for her life. Now she was entrusted with spiritual motherhood, having been prepared for this by God over the course of the years through the painful separation from her Son and through all the wounds inflicted upon her.

After Mary was comforted by the love of the dying Lord, the agonizing cry came from His lips, "My God, my God, why hast thou forsaken me?" This was the last and most terrible suffering that Mary had to share with Jesus in her soul. A cry would also have welled up in her: "Where is my God now? Yes, my

God, You have forsaken me — You who led me along these paths!" Her soul would have been one great cry of despair. If Jesus as the Son of God cried out, "My God, my God, why hast thou forsaken me?" would not Mary, who as a frail human being was far more liable to doubts and temptations, have cried out at this outcome of God's promises and purposes, "My God, my God, what have You done?" Hopelessness, agony and death were all that remained.

But then she heard Jesus' words, "It is finished!" and that which only He, the Son of God, could say, "Father, into thy hands I commit my spirit!" After saying this, He breathed His last. Was she at all capable of taking in these final words of His or did they merely reach her heart from afar? Standing beneath the cross, she probably could not yet comprehend what had happened: the Son of God had accomplished His work.

Yes, for Jesus everything had been led to a conclusion: His work had been completed; the words, "It is finished!" were a reality. But Mary and His disciples were left behind in grief and despair that death had triumphed. It is impossible to imagine what must have been going on in the heart of the mother Mary when the One she loved above all else, the Son of God, her Child, hung dead on the cross. To her it would have seemed that His enemies had been victorious and His life-work lay in ruins. He had been disposed of and His kingdom had come to an end. He had not become the king and ruler of Israel, and all the pathways followed in obedience to God's promises had ended in meaninglessness. There was a sense of finality about it all. Draining the cup of suffering, she tasted the last bitter dregs.

The sword pierces deep; the wound in His side
Declares now to sinners: the Saviour has died;
For my sake my Lord had to suffer.
His blood freely flows from the wound in His side,
That sinners salvation and healing may find
In the blood of the Lamb, pure and holy.

And he who is close to the heart of our Lord
Is called to feel with Him the thrust of the sword,
The pain that is caused by our sinning.
Now we may find life in the pure crimson flood
Which flows from the side of the Lamb of God.
By His holy blood we are healed.

And Mary, devoted in love to her Lord,
Bore with Him the pain and the thrust of the sword.
Her own heart was rent by its piercing.
The bleeding wound, burning and searing with pain,
Was felt in her own soul again and again,
Imprinted there many times over.

O Mary, what sorrow and anguish you bore!
We thank you for having stood with our Lord
And willingly borne all the torment.
We want to stand with you beneath Jesus' cross,
In spirit bear with Him His pain, grief, and loss,
United with Him in His suffering.

All these with one accord devoted themselves to prayer, together with the women and Mary the mother of Jesus, and with his brothers.

Acts 1:14

Because Mary had shared in the depths of Jesus' sufferings on His way to the cross, her experience of

110

Easter and Pentecost must have been all the greater. In the Acts of the Apostles we read of how she prayed and waited for the promised coming of the Holy Spirit. If previously her life was characterized by her special calling as mother of Jesus, now she shared in the fellowship of the disciples and had a place in the body of believers, which though still in embryo was the fruit of her Son's sacrificial death. Together with the disciples she humbly waited for the coming of the Holy Spirit, the promised Comforter, although the Holy Spirit had already drawn so close to her when, as the power of the Highest, He overshadowed her. But now a new birth was to take place, a spiritual one, the birth of the Body of Christ.

The path that she had trodden with Jesus as His mother was completed. Now she waited for the infilling of the Holy Spirit. What a wonderful Pentecost the Lord must have prepared for her! But her joy at the coming of the Spirit in fulfilment of God's promise was but a foretaste of the joy she would reap in the heavenly world for all eternity when every one of God's promises are fulfilled at last.

Yes, the words can be applied to her, "Blessed are you that weep now, for you shall laugh" (Luke 6:21). Joyful laughter will now be her lot for all eternity and she will join in celebrating Jesus' victory, the redemption He wrought, His dominion over Israel and over all the nations of the earth. She will rejoice and raise songs of praise that all of God's promises are being gloriously fulfilled along paths of deepest suffering.

The greater the calling, the greater the suffering. And so it was inevitable that her life was consummated in the fullness of suffering. She was immersed in suffering, but for this reason she will also be

111

privileged to taste the fullness of glory. If on earth she suffered immeasurably because her Son, instead of receiving the promised kingship, endured nothing but disgrace, how she will rejoice now in the heavenly glory to see Jesus worshipped and honoured at the throne of God! And having personally received the promise of His dominion over Israel she will surely rejoice more than anyone else, giving thanks and worshipping Him, when His people finally acknowledge Jesus as their king and pay Him homage.

Yes, if we partake in the sufferings of Jesus, we shall also partake in His glory. This is the testimony of Holy Scripture: "If we endure, we shall also reign with him" (2 Timothy 2:12) and "...provided we suffer with him in order that we may also be glorified with him" (Romans 8:17). In regal splendour the mother Mary will now be permitted to dwell at His throne, for He "has made us kings and priests to his God and Father" (Revelation 1:6 RAV). Now she will continually behold Him whom her soul loves and for whose sake her heart was pierced by a sword, and she will reign with Him as Scripture has promised for those who overcome (Revelation 3:21).

Epilogue

Martin Luther said of the mother Mary:

What are all the maidservants, manservants, gentlemen, ladies, princes, kings, monarchs on earth compared with the Virgin Mary, who is of royal lineage and, moreover, the mother of God,* the noblest lady on earth? After Christ she is the fairest gem in all of Christendom. Never can she be praised enough: the supreme empress and queen, far exalted above all nobility, wisdom and holiness.[2]

* See also in *Formula of Concord*: "Therefore we believe, teach, and confess that Mary…is rightly called, and truly is, the mother of God."[1]

How fitting it would have been if a golden carriage had been ordered for her, escorted by four thousand horses and with a messenger leading the way, sounding the trumpet and crying with a loud voice, "Here comes the noblest of ladies, the princess of all mankind!" But nothing of the sort happened. Instead the poor maiden journeys such a long way on foot, although she already is the mother of God. It would have been no wonder if all the mountains had leapt and danced for joy.[3]

Hence men have crowded all her glory into a single word, calling her the Mother of God. No one can say anything greater of her or to her, though he had as many tongues as there are leaves on the trees, or grass in the fields, or stars in the sky, or sand by the sea. It needs to be pondered in the heart what it means to be the Mother of God.[4]

Reading these words of Martin Luther, who revered the mother Mary to the end of his life, observed the festivals of the Virgin Mary, and daily sang the Magnificat, we can sense how far the majority of us have drifted away from the proper attitude towards her, which Martin Luther has indicated to us on the basis of Holy Scripture. The influence of rationalism is all too evident among us Protestants, affecting our way of thinking, although such phrases as the following can be found in the Confessions of the Evangelical Lutheran Church: Mary is "worthy of the highest honours".[5]

Rationalism had lost the sense of the sacred. The holy things of God are too far removed from earthly concepts to be grasped by human reason. When we cross the threshold of this holy sphere, we can only bow down in awe and adoration. In rationalism man sought to comprehend everything, and that which he could not comprehend he rejected. In contrast, Scripture is aware of the mystery surrounding the holy things of God and is cautious in dealing with them. Instead of dissecting everything, it treats such matters very discreetly and with great delicacy. And so it should not surprise us that little is written about the mother Mary. Is it not sufficient that the one vital fact is attested? She had to do with the most holy of all; the Son of God Himself was born of her as a human being and was her Child. She is thus included in the sphere of the holy things of God.

Only he who has not lost that sense of awe and wonder when coming into contact with something holy, only he who removes his shoes when treading holy ground, just as Joshua did at the appearance of the Prince of the Lord's host (Joshua 5:15), will have an inkling of the mystery about the mother Mary. He will be able to grasp, though but dimly, what a miracle it was that a member of our sinful human race was privileged to become the mother of the Son of God. But because rationalism accepted only that which could be explained rationally, Church festivals in honour of Mary and everything else reminiscent of her were done away with in the Protestant Church. All biblical relationship to the mother Mary was lost, and we are still suffering from this heritage.

When Martin Luther bids us to praise the mother Mary, declaring that she can never be praised enough as the noblest lady and, after Christ, the fairest gem in Christendom, I must confess that for many years I was one of those who had not done so, although Scripture says that henceforth all generations would call Mary blessed (Luke 1:48). I had not taken my place among these generations. To be sure, I had read in Scripture how Elizabeth, that woman favoured by God, prophesied by the Holy Spirit and addressed Mary as "the mother of my Lord". Indeed, she showed Mary the utmost honour, saying to her kinswoman, so much younger than her, "Why is this granted me, that the mother of my Lord should come to me?" And so truly I could have learnt from Elizabeth's example what the right attitude was. However, I did not honour the mother Mary with a single thought, word or song, let alone consider her to be someone who, in the words of Luther, can never be praised enough.

When writing this book about the life of the

mother Mary, as we know it from the Bible, I was conscious of an obligation, having failed to do as the Word of God says. By the grace of the Lord I have in the past few decades increasingly learnt to love and revere the mother Mary the more I contemplated her life on the basis of Holy Scripture. It is my prayer that the Lord may use this book so that among us Protestants Mary, the mother of our Lord, will once again receive the love and honour that are her due according to Holy Scripture and as the reformer Martin Luther has impressed upon our hearts.

At this point I would like to acknowledge gratefully how I have been blessed by the testimony of her obedience, total commitment, and willingness to accept difficult leadings, trials and hardships. Because she led a life of lowliness in this spirit of complete surrender, "the tender mother of Christ", as Luther says in his exposition of the Magnificat, "teaches us with her words and by the example of her experience, how to know, love, and praise God".[6]

Should there not be thanksgiving in our hearts towards Mary? With her Yes she was privileged to bring us the Son of God, Jesus Christ, the Salvation of the world, who re-opened for us the gates of paradise. Considering what she has given us, should we not love her? Among us Protestants the Apostles Paul and Peter are regarded with great love. Often we feel very close to them spiritually, thanking and honouring them for their lives of discipleship. We give thanks to the Apostle Paul, knowing that if it were not for him the message of Jesus would not have reached us, the Gentile nations. Filled with gratitude, we praise the martyrs, whose blood is the seed of the Church. Yet how often we forget to thank the mother Mary!

116

Is she not counted among the "cloud of witnesses" who are about us (Hebrews 12:1) and whose testimony is meant to strengthen us for the race that we have to run? If we honour the apostles and archangels and take them for our guides by calling our churches after them, how can we exclude Mary, who was the first to share Jesus' way of the cross and who as His mother was so close to Him?

In our Protestant Church honour and praise were largely denied her out of fear of diminishing the honour of Jesus. But whenever proper honour is shown to her, or to any other disciple of Jesus for that matter, the honour of the Lord is magnified, for He it is who chose her, favoured her, and made her His vessel. Her faith, love, and dedication, all of which were directed towards God, serve to make Him the centre and glorify Him.

And so it is our desire as the Evangelical Sisterhood of Mary* to do as Holy Scripture says and not grieve our Lord Jesus with an irreverent attitude towards the mother Mary or by disregarding her. For she is His mother, who bore and reared Him and of whom the Holy Spirit, speaking through Elizabeth, said, "Blessed is she who believed."

---

* As a result of a revival among the Girls' Bible Study Groups in Darmstadt following the destruction of the city at the end of World War II, Mother Basilea Schlink founded the Evangelical Sisterhood of Mary within the frame of the German Protestant State Church. The ministry grew and the little Land of Canaan was established in Darmstadt, West Germany. Now there are Canaan centres in over 20 countries. The Evangelical Sisterhood of Mary is an international, interdenominational organization.

Jesus is waiting for us to honour and love Mary. This is what God's Word tells us and thus it is His will that we do so, for only those who keep His Word love Him truly (John 14:23).

Praise to the mother Mary,
The mother of our Lord,
The pure and lowly handmaid.
Love, honour we accord.
With Elizabeth we praise for
What God for her has done.
She trusted in His promise
And brought to us the Son.

Praise to the mother Mary,
The mother of our Lord,
The pure and lowly handmaid.
Love, honour we accord.
She gave her Yes, said humbly,
"So be it unto me",
And trod the lone, dark pathway
That led to Calvary.

Praise to the mother Mary,
The mother of our Lord,
The pure and lowly handmaid.
Love, honour we accord.
She bore temptations, trials,
Great pain and inner night,
When she saw no fulfilment
Of what was prophesied.

Praise to the mother Mary,
The mother of our Lord,
The pure and lowly handmaid.
Love, honour we accord.
As Scripture has commanded,
We call you blessed today;

With grateful hearts we praise Him
For your great trust and faith.

Praise to the mother Mary,
The mother of our Lord,
The pure and lowly handmaid.
Love, honour we accord.
Because you were so humble
God raised you up so high;
For this with joy we praise Him,
His glory magnify.

Notes

1 Martin Luther, "Formula of Concord, Article VIII, Section 7", in *The Book of Concord*, ed. and trans. Theodore G. Tappert (Philadelphia: Fortress Press, 1959), p.488

2 Martin Luther, "Predigten an Weihnachten, oder heiligem Christfest, Isaiah 9:2-7, Erste Predigt, 1532", in *Dr. Martin Luther's Hauspostille*, Vol. 6 of *Dr. Martin Luther's Sämmtliche Werke*, ed. Joh. Georg Plochmann (Erlangen: Verlag von Carl Hender, 1826), p.48

3 Martin Luther, "Predigten am Tage der Heimsuchung Mariä, Luke 1:39-56, Erste Predigt, 1533", in *Dr. Martin Luther's Hauspostille*, Vol. 6 of *Dr. Martin Luther's Sämmtliche Werke*, ed. Joh. Georg Plochmann (Erlangen: Verlag von Carl Hender, 1826), p.303

4 Martin Luther, "The Magnificat", in *Luther's Works*, Vol. 21, trans. A.T.W. Steinhaeuser, ed. Jaroslav Pelikan (Saint Louis: Concordia Publishing House, 1956), p.326

5 Martin Luther, "Apology of the Augsburg Confession, Article XXI, Section 27", in *The Book of Concord*, ed. and trans. Theodore G. Tappert (Philadelphia: Fortress Press, 1959), p.232

6 Martin Luther, "The Magnificat", in *Luther's Works*, Vol. 21, trans. A.T.W. Steinhaeuser, ed. Jaroslav Pelikan (Saint Louis: Concordia Publishing House, 1956), p.301

Other books by Basilea Schlink
for your further interest

IN WHOM THE FATHER DELIGHTS   96 pp.
There are times in our lives when God's leadings
seem hard to understand and the heart cries out,
"Why did it have to happen to me? It's almost break-
ing me!" Loneliness, perhaps. Disappointments. A
marriage on the rocks. Severe illness and disable-
ment. Or emotional stress... Yet never are we so dear
to our heavenly Father as when we are undergoing
trials and chastenings. As a wise and loving Father
He brings us up carefully, desiring only the very best
for us. And if we trustingly put our hand in His, we
shall find that He has prepared a wonderful outcome
to every path of suffering.

MY ALL FOR HIM   160 pp.
In this book is described first-hand, vital, all-de-
manding discipleship, but not as an ideal possible
only to the few — for it depends not upon our abilities
but upon our Lord's love burning in our hearts.
"I just had to write to tell you how much your book
My All for Him means to me. I cannot go one day
without it and take it everywhere with me on my
trips. It is the most beautiful book I have ever read,
and I long for a deeper understanding of this Bridal
Love."
"Your book aroused and increased my love for Jesus
with each page read and made me feel His reality viv-
idly."

BEHOLD HIS LOVE   144 pp.

Nothing can bring us closer to Jesus than meditating upon His Passion, for in doing so we search the depths of His heart. This book will help us to find a warm, vital relationship with our Saviour when we behold His amazing love which compelled Him to choose suffering and death for our sakes.

RULED BY THE SPIRIT   132 pp.

As in the days of the early Church, described in the Book of Acts, the power of God to guide and inspire individuals who dedicate their lives wholly to Him is still operative today; this is the kernel of Basilea Schlink's challenging message in this book.

I FOUND THE KEY TO THE
HEART OF GOD

Autobiography, 416 pp. illustrated

We turn the pages as we would the score of some great symphony and whether the music is light or whether it is the deep chords that are struck, our hearts cannot fail to respond. The response will be an inner searching of our own hearts and lives followed by love and adoration for our Lord Jesus. The reader seeking a greater fulfilment in his Christian life and service will discover in these pages the key to the very heart of God.

THE HIDDEN TREASURE IN SUFFERING
96 pp.

Cares — Strained Relationships — Fear — Illness — Weariness — Loneliness — Inner Conflict — Personality Problems — Unanswered Prayers — Untalented — Growing Old — Want and Need — Fear of Death — Unfair Treatment — Facing Hatred and Slander...

From the wealth of her personal experience Mother Basilea Schlink shares how we can find the treasure that lies hidden in every trial and hardship.

THE UNSEEN WORLD OF ANGELS AND DEMONS   144 pp.

Whether we realize it or not, we are caught up in a colossal battle between light and darkness, good and evil. Neutrality is impossible, for the battle is being fought over us.

Basing her work on the Bible and illustrating her points with many testimonies, Mother Basilea exposes the sinister, destructive purposes of Satan and his demon hordes for mankind. At the same time she depicts the ministry of God's angels. Though we may not usually be aware of their presence, angels are constantly about us, helping, protecting, guiding. They play an active role in human affairs, influencing men and nations, yes, the very course of history.

This book not only shows how they will help us to win the victory in these dark times, but also gives us a glimpse of the love, power, and glory of God as reflected in His holy angels.

REPENTANCE – THE JOY-FILLED LIFE
96 pp.
A remarkable little volume, showing how an attitude
of repentance affects a Christian's inner and outer
life.

YOU WILL NEVER BE THE SAME
192 pp.
How can we overcome sin? Asked this question,
Basilea Schlink set about prescribing "spiritual
medicine", dealing one by one with the sinful traits
which mar the Christian's life, helping us to recognize
them in ourselves, and pointing out the remedy. We
can be transformed by gaining victory over our sins in
the power of Jesus Christ, our risen Lord and
Saviour.

FATHER OF COMFORT
(Daily Readings)   128 pp.
These short devotions for every day of the year help
us to develop that close contact, a personal relationship of love and childlike trust in the Father, which
we need in order to nurture our faith in Him.
"That book has helped me like nothing in this world!
I have bought 12 copies and sent them to various
friends all over the world. I can't tell you how it has
spoken to my rebellious heart, gotten my eyes off
people and on to Jesus."

Penny - pray that my immune cells
would become too
cancer cancer cell &
that I may be a faithful
friend to Pam Henderson
whose I know died
this week.

Karen S. - David missed passing a
8th. test. last fail. needs
this testing after re-exam
in mid-April.

Terry M - Lauren needs a job
& wisdom. Better att.
for Terry & Jason needs
healing.

Chris. - husband has had 102°
temp. needs healing from
flu.